THE WAY TO LIFE
Understanding the Gospel Message

THE WAY TO LIFE
Understanding the Gospel Message

Aaron J. Carey

Living Faith Books

Apprehending Truth Publishers
Brookfield, Missouri
2012

THE WAY TO LIFE
Understanding the Gospel Message

by

Aaron J. Carey

Copyright © 2012 by Aaron Carey
This book is non-copyright. Free distribution is encouraged.

ISBN-13: 978-0615741109
ISBN-10: 061574110X

"All Scripture is taken from the King James Version. Some words have been updated to clarify contemporary meaning. The author has underlined certain passages for emphasis."

Cover Design by PureLight Graphics

Living Faith Books is an imprint of:
Apprehending Truth Publishers
PO Box 249
Brookfield, Missouri 64628
http://www.ApprehendingTruth.net

The Way To Life:
Understanding The Gospel Message

Contents:

CHAPTER 1:
 THE ESSENTIAL MESSAGE OF JOHN THE BAPTIST
　　　　　　　　　　　　　　　　　　　　　　1

CHAPTER 2:
 THE ESSENTIAL MESSAGE OF JOHN THE BAPTIST
(CONTINUED)　　　　　　　　　　　　　　　6

CHAPTER 3:
CHRIST HAS MADE A WAY THROUGH THE CROSS
　　　　　　　　　　　　　　　　　　　　　29

CHAPTER 4:
BEING IN CHRIST MEANS BEING IN THE KINGDOM
OF GOD　　　　　　　　　　　　　　　　　38

CHAPTER 5:
SOBRIETY: AN ESSENTIAL OF TRUE CHRISTIANITY
　　　　　　　　　　　　　　　　　　　　　70

Chapter 1:
The Essential Message Of John The Baptist

"The beginning of the gospel of Jesus Christ, the Son of God; As it is written in the prophets, Behold, I send my messenger before thy face, which shall prepare thy way before thee. The voice of one crying in the wilderness, Prepare ye the way of the Lord, make his paths straight. John did baptize in the wilderness, and preach the baptism of repentance for the remission of sins." (Mark 1:1-4)

The final preparation for Christ before he appeared on Israel's national scene and began his public ministry was so important because about 400 years had passed in which there had not been a prophet in Israel. That is approximately the length of time it's been since the Pilgrims first came to America! That is the time span between the Old and New Testaments. During that time Israel was indeed awaiting the promised Messiah, the ruler and deliverer that had been spoken of repeatedly in their scriptures. Those scriptures also spoke of the messenger whom God would send to directly prepare Israel for the Lord's coming- which was in reality a message intended to restore the Israelites to the heart they should have had toward God had they then been molded by the word of God instead of their own hearts and the traditions of men. This messenger is John the Baptist.

"Behold, I will send my messenger, and he shall prepare the way before me: and the Lord, whom ye seek, shall suddenly come to his temple, even the messenger of the covenant, whom ye delight in: behold, he shall come, saith the Lord of hosts." (Malachi 3:1)

"The voice of him that cries in the wilderness, Prepare ye the way of the Lord, make straight in the desert a highway for our God." (Isaiah 40:3)

All Must Believe Through John

John the Baptist's message is just as important for us as well. **"There was a man sent from God, whose name was John. The same came for a witness, to bear witness of the Light, <u>that all men through him might believe</u>. He was not that Light, but was sent to bear witness of that Light." (John 1:6-8)**

The gospel of John constantly emphasizes Jesus as the Son of God and belief in him as the way to eternal life. Yet John (the Apostle- a different John than John the Baptist) who wrote the gospel of John makes it very clear at the beginning that responding to John the Baptist's witness is necessary to believe on Jesus Christ, who is the true and ultimate light. **"In him** (Christ) **was life; and the life was the light of men." (John 1:4)** Reject John the Baptist's message and you reject the one on whose behalf he spoke. Jesus affirmed this regarding John the Baptist when some of Israel's leaders openly challenged his authority (see Matthew 21:23-32). Had these men rightly responded to John the Baptist they would not have been defiant to Jesus. A right response to John is necessary to have a right response to Jesus. We saw above that all who truly believe do so through John.

This has not changed today. Though Jesus is now

casually presented to people for salvation and people seem to easily respond to this casual gospel presentation it cannot be a true response to Jesus Christ as he is revealed in scripture, the real Jesus, unless the message of John the Baptist is responded to. Hence the shallowness and futility of many professions of faith in Jesus Christ today, as well as a widespread misunderstanding of his gospel of salvation; and with that a great misunderstanding and confusion over what it actually means to have salvation in Christ. For though John the Baptist has died and is with the Lord his message never changes. He was sent to **"prepare the way of the Lord"** as we saw. Salvation is Jesus Christ himself, who is the Lord (Luke 2:11) and he cannot just come casually to one whose heart is not in agreement with his purpose. **"And thou shalt call his name Jesus: for he shall save his people from their sins." (Matthew 1:21b)** The heart of a person must be turned to Christ's way and only then can he come to save one. Two must be agreed to walk together (Amos 3:3) and Jesus must lead, and not vice-versa, in order for us to be joined to him by saving faith. To bring us to this agreement is the intended function of the message of John the Baptist.

Thus John the Baptist's father Zacharias, inspired by God's Spirit, spoke of him at his birth **"And thou, child, shall be called the prophet of the Highest: for thou shalt go before the face of the Lord to prepare his ways; To give knowledge of salvation unto his people by the remission of their sins, Through the tender mercy of our God; whereby the dayspring** (i.e. the light of dawn) **from on high has visited us, To give light to them that sit in darkness and in the shadow of death, to guide our feet into the way of peace." (Luke 1:76-79)**

A Key Question Considered

Can Jesus Christ be received by someone without their specifically reading or hearing the words of John the Baptist recorded in the gospels? Yes, it's possible. <u>It's really about the message God spoke through John the Baptist as a preparation for Christ which He reiterated through the preaching of Jesus and the Apostles, and continues to reiterate in all true gospel preaching</u> . Jesus and the Apostles reiterated the message of John the Baptist, as will any faithful witness of Jesus Christ who is sent of God today. John the Baptist, Jesus himself (for our sakes), and the Apostles all called people to Jesus. We emphasize John the Baptist's message here because the gospel writers did so at the beginning of the gospels and clearly state that the beginning of the gospel of Jesus Christ is the preaching of John the Baptist and that all must believe through John, as we have seen (Mark 1:1-4, John 1:6-8).

We can easily open the gospels and disregard John's message, which is highlighted early on in all four gospel accounts, as something "to just get through quickly" in order to get to Jesus' public ministry. This is a great error though since it is the wisdom of God that we heed John's message first. Many think they have received Jesus who are not heeding the message of John which is essential to heed in order to prepare the way for Jesus, the salvation of God, to dwell in us.

It is true that we should follow Jesus, not John the Baptist. Absolutely true. However we cannot follow Jesus until we hear and obey the message of John. It cannot be set aside. We have seen that this preaching of John is <u>the</u> God-ordained preparation in order for His Christ to be received and it sets a pattern and a precedent for every other gospel preacher in the New Testament and subsequently for true gospel preaching until the end of this age. So we need to open our ears, listen carefully to that message, and respond!

Chapter 2:
The Essential Message of John the Baptist (Continued)

Luke chapter 3 contains a very thorough account of John the Baptist's message which contains most of what the other gospel writers include. We'll simply go through that and add what is necessary to add regarding John the Baptist here from other places in scripture that we haven't looked at already. The words of John the Baptist and the words that are directly about him in this chapter are put in italics to distinguish them from other scriptures which we'll look at that compliment and confirm them.

Preparing the Way Of the Lord

"And he came into all the country about Jordan, preaching the baptism of repentance for the remission of sins; As it is written in the book of the words of Esaias (Isaiah) *the prophet, saying, The voice of one crying in the wilderness, Prepare ye the way of the Lord, make his paths straight." (Luke 3:3-4)*

This message preaches the baptism of repentance for the remission of sins to prepare the way for Jesus Christ, the salvation of God.

Always, in both the Old and New Testaments, is repentance the condition of remission of sins (same as forgiveness of sins). Forgiveness of sins is something that God could give even before the cross, knowing that Christ would **"taste death for every man." (Hebrews 2:9b)** God's forgiveness has always been only for those who fear Him (meaning fear to offend Him, honor His authority as God- not merely fear His punishment and hell). **"The secret of the Lord is with them that fear him; and he will shew them his covenant." (Psalm 25:14) "For as the heaven is high above the earth, so great is his mercy toward them that fear him." (Psalm 103:11)**

By seeing the characteristic of the fear of God we can understand what repentance is- for repentance and the fear of the Lord cannot be separated from each other. **"Be not wise in thine own eyes: fear the Lord, and depart from evil." (Proverbs 3:7) "The fear of the Lord is to hate evil" (Proverbs 8:13a) "By mercy and truth iniquity is purged: and by the fear of the Lord** *men* **depart from evil." (Proverbs 16:6)**

Many today preach repentance as (merely) a change of mind, being sorry, admitting you're a sinner, to trust Jesus and not yourself to go to heaven, etc. Yet none of these are the Bible's definition of repentance. The Bible never changed the definition of repentance from the Old to New Testament so we do not have a right to either (Jesus actually illustrated the repentance we must respond to him with by the Old Testament example of the people of the city of Nineveh in the book of Jonah- Matthew 12:41).

To truly repent we must turn to the Lord and bow under His authority; and in so turning forsake our transgressions of His commandments. To despise God's commandment is to despise His authority- which is actually despising Him. We see this in the words of Nathan the Prophet as he reproved King David on God's behalf in the Old Testament:

"Wherefore hast thou <u>despised the commandment of the Lord</u>, to do evil in his sight? thou hast killed Uriah the Hittite with the sword, and hast taken his wife to be thy wife, and hast slain him with the sword of the children of Ammon. Now therefore the sword shall never depart from thine house; because <u>thou hast despised me</u>, and hast taken the wife of Uriah the Hittite to be thy wife." (2 Samuel 12:9-10)

Repentance then is turning from/forsaking the sin which separates us from God, as any and all willful sin separates the willful sinner from God (willful sin is sin a person refuses to forsake). **"Behold, the Lord's hand is not shortened, that it cannot save; neither his ear heavy, that it cannot hear: But your iniquities have separated between you and your God, and your sins have hid his face from you, that he will not hear." (Isaiah 59:1-2).** We can clearly see how God called people to repentance in the Old Testament:

"Therefore I will judge you, O house of Israel, every one according to his ways, saith the Lord God. Repent, and turn yourselves from <u>all</u> your transgressions; so iniquity shall not be your ruin. Cast away from you <u>all</u> your transgressions, whereby you have transgressed; and make you a new heart and a new spirit: for why will you die, O house of Israel? For I have no pleasure in the death of him that dies, says the Lord God: wherefore turn yourselves, and live ye." (Ezekiel 18:30-32).

"Seek ye the Lord while he may be found, call ye upon him while he is near: Let the wicked forsake his way, and the unrighteous man his thoughts: and let him return unto the Lord, and he will have mercy upon him; and to our God, for he will abundantly pardon."

(Isaiah 55:6-7)

We should also note that submitting to water baptism was preached with repentance by John, as well as by Jesus and the Apostles. We'll shortly touch on the reason for this. We see repentance with submission to water baptism preached by the Apostles after the cross as the condition to receiving Jesus Christ and His Spirit (Acts 2:38), which we'll also deal with more eventually.

The Outcome Of Repentance

"Every valley shall be filled, and every mountain and hill shall be brought low; and the crooked shall be made straight, and the rough ways shall be made smooth; And all flesh shall see the salvation of God." (Luke 3:5-6)

The valleys, mountains/hills, crooked, and rough ways all clearly symbolize the low, high, crooked, and/or rough nature of the many different sins that can be willfully committed and held onto. Whatever sin there is, whether it be respectable or shameful in the eyes of society- or out of sight from people altogether- must be forsaken for Jesus the salvation of God to come to us. It is in Christ coming to an individual in power and in one thus partaking of his life by his dwelling in them that is true salvation. This partaking of Christ's life necessarily results in a demonstration of his righteousness by the transformation which reconciliation and union with the Lord of the Universe, whose great concern is to save us from our sins, necessarily brings. The Apostle Paul would testify **"For I am not ashamed of the gospel of Christ: for it is the power of God unto salvation to every one that believes; to the Jew first, and also to the Greek. For therein is the righteousness of God revealed from faith to faith: as it is written, The just**

shall live by faith." (Romans 1:16-17)

Not A Politically Correct Message

"Then said he to the multitude that came forth to be baptized of him, O generation of vipers, who hath warned you to flee from the wrath to come?" (Luke 3:7)

The message of John identifies the devilish characteristic of unrepentant mankind and warns the unrepentant to flee from the wrath to come. Though there are carnal men who arrogantly try to imitate this type of language in self-righteous pride, it is nevertheless the language God's word uses. There is such a thing as a severe rebuke being the kindest, most loving thing that can be said. Those who say such words without love can do much damage, but we must go beyond those and hear the true rebuke and warning of God's word- which are indeed given in love.

Fleeing from the wrath to come, as we looked at, means turning to the Lord in repentance- a repentance which forsakes sin so thoroughly that it strikes at the very root of sin, which is enmity against God's authority. All willful sin springs from this enmity. This enmity can be shown by open hostility towards God but it can also be evidenced by a casual apathy towards what God has commanded as well as apathy in seeking to know what God has said about something- basically an attitude of "whatever" or "who cares" towards life's choices in relation to God's commandments. This enmity can even appear reverent in a deceitful way. If a child is told by his father that he wants him to mow the lawn and stay out of the cookies before dinner and the child nods and says "Sure dad, I love you" and then goes and mows the lawn yet nevertheless steals cookies before dinner, he is in truth a rebellious and disobedient towards his father's authority.

If he goes and does another chore to make up for eating the forbidden cookies, he is still rebellious and disobedient. And he remains so until he turns to his father at heart and renounces ever thinking he could despise him in anything at all and that it would be good and okay to do so.

The key differences are that most reading this are fully accountable to God unlike a very young child who isn't; and God's authority and goodness are infinitely greater than the best parent's (though to honor God we certainly must honor His command to honor our father and mother). It also should be said that though some parents might be cruel to their children and command things that are truly wrong and/or unreasonable, the Lord by His very nature never would or could do so[1]. Those who think they can do what God has forbidden in any way and/or not do all they are obligated by Him to do basically put themselves in God's place and assert the reign over their lives in defiance of Him. Consider a person proclaiming him/herself to be God. No doubt that's exceedingly evil beyond words. Yet that's what those who go their own way and deny God's authority over their lives essentially do, though most would never say so with their lips.

Fruits Which Demonstrate Repentance Are Necessary

"Bring forth therefore fruits worthy of repentance, and begin not to say within yourselves, We have Abraham to our father: for I say unto you, That God is able of these stones to raise up children unto Abraham." (Luke 3:8)

---

[1] Some parents also spoil or neglect their children and don't even command them what is right and reasonable.

The message of John insists on fruit meet (fit) for repentance and cuts down all vain confidences which excuse the lack of this. It is one thing to say you repent, but quite another to actually pay the price to obey God. We see later in Luke that Zacchaeus the tax collector had to forsake a large amount of his wealth in order to pay back those whom he had defrauded and tear his heart from the love of money. **"And Zacchaeus stood, and said unto the Lord: Behold, Lord, the half of my goods I give to the poor; and if I have taken any thing from any man by false accusation, I restore him fourfold. And Jesus said unto him, This day is salvation come to this house, forasmuch as he also is a son of Abraham. For the Son of man is come to seek and to save that which was lost. " (Luke 19:8-10).**

It's clear that Jesus knew this man's heart and knew he truly was fully set to go through with his words and make things right no matter the cost. Only in this did Jesus say that salvation had come to Zacchaeus' house. He heeded the message of John and thus could receive Jesus in truth. Thus Jesus the salvation of God came to his house.

Many would wrongly call this working to earn one's salvation, but this is not talking about paying the debt for one's sins (which only what Christ suffered on the cross can do). Rather this is simply about honoring God's authority- regarding which Christ's death for our sins was with the purpose of bringing rebels back under. If a man was committing adultery and went to ask his wife for forgiveness, would he not need to break off the adulterous relationship or else his asking for forgiveness would be a mockery to his wife? Of course he would need to end the adulterous relationship though there may be a great price to pay. The pleasure and the attachment of the adulterous relationship need to be cut off no matter how painful the consequences of doing so. Sin can be very advantageous and pleasurable FOR THE MOMENT but to side with Christ we must, like Moses, forsake the pleasures of sin and enter into the affliction that the true people of God suffer for the sake of obedience to God (see Hebrews 11:24-26). The man is not paying a price to buy his wife's favor; he is paying the necessary price to honor the husband/wife relationship.

The Bible condemns the things people do and give to attempt to earn God's favor; yet it insists that God's authority as Creator and Ruler of the universe who has a full, non-transferrable right to our worship and obedience be honored by His creation. (Does not the one who tries to bribe forgiveness out of someone likely do so in attempt to avoid the necessary terms of the relationship- whether towards a spouse, a government, or towards the Lord?) Why do many think then that God's honor is less and that He can be dishonored in a way that no sane person, even a genuinely merciful one, ever should/could allow themselves to be? All who think they can be forgiven without bringing forth fruit worthy of repentance so mock God. We see how the Apostle Paul preached this same truth in his gospel preaching after Christ had appeared to him as well. **"Whereupon, O king Agrippa, I was not disobedient unto the heavenly vision: But showed first unto them of Damascus, and at Jerusalem, and throughout all the coasts of Judaea, and then to the Gentiles, that they should repent and turn to God, and do works meet** (fit) **for repentance." (Acts 26:19-20).**

False Confidence Reproved

In Luke 3:8 we also see a warning not to trust in a false hope that excuses fruits worthy for repentance in our life. The Jews of the time believed that since God had made a covenant with Abraham their direct ancestor that they were therefore automatically in a covenant with God and safe from His wrath. John warned not to think this *"within yourselves"* for God could raise up true children to Abraham (those that walk by faith in obedience to God) among those who are not Abraham's physical descendants (represented by stones). *"Within yourselves"* is a key phrase. People didn't say it out loud normally. So now it's easy to say in one's heart "I go to church" "I give money to charity" "I was raised in a loving, Christian home" "I'm a descendant of (whoever)" "I did (whatever)" and for things like this we can easily take a false comfort that we are safe from God's wrath. This false comfort and confidence can even come from having "accepted Jesus" IF we are not bringing forth fruit fit for repentance and subject to his word NOW (we'll deal with this in greater detail in chapter 4).

Those who take such false confidence will not heed the warning to flee from the wrath to come and bring forth fruits worthy of repentance as they ought to. It cannot and will not truly be done without urgency and diligence. Hearing the message of John means the end of all confidence in things which excuse the need for repentance toward God and bringing forth the fruit which must accompany that.

The importance of submitting to water baptism in repentance is the true acknowledgment that one is turning from a life of disobedience to a life of obedience to God, a true acknowledgment that you must be made new and thus now have no confidence in anything from your former life. However getting baptized as a formality and/or to join a church has no profit.

The Axe At The Roots And Eternal Judgment

"And now also the axe is laid unto the root of the

trees: every tree therefore which brings not forth good fruit is hewn down, and cast into the fire." (Luke 3:9)

This aspect of the message of John speaks for itself and there is no way around it. It is possible also to flatter ourselves that some people are (allegedly) worse than we are and therefore excuse sin in our lives. However the word of God says that everyone who doesn't repent of sin at its very root of denying God"s authority over their lives and who isn't (presently) bringing forth fruit in keeping with repentance is in as great danger of hell-fire as a tree is of falling that has an axe laid at its root. A tree which only the patience of God prevents from being struck and chopped down. This patience is limited. The Apostle Paul would write **"Or despisest thou the riches of his goodness and forbearance** (restraint) **and long-suffering** (patience)**; not knowing that the goodness of God leads thee to repentance? But after thy hardness and impenitent heart treasurest up unto thyself wrath against the day of wrath and revelation of the righteous judgment of God" (Romans 2:4-5)**

The necessity of bearing good fruit is affirmed by Jesus and the Apostles repeatedly as necessary to enter God's kingdom, as we have already seen in multiple Bible passages and will see from more. We can wrongly use Bible passages about salvation being by faith and not works, not understanding what faith is or what type of works we are referring to (see the first section on Luke 3:8 given earlier). There is such a thing as a dead faith, which even the devils have (James 2:19). This faith does not produce living works which God approves of. There are also dead works (Hebrews 6:1) that are not done out of faith/obedience toward God, but rather stem from keeping the traditions of men, as well as works done in unbelief to impress other people and/or works done to merely get the duty done so one can go on with their own life. A living faith ALWAYS results in living works done out of obedience to God which glorify Him. James 2:14-26 makes this truth absolutely clear beyond any doubt. Here is why it is absolutely necessary to seek God through how He has made Himself known in the Bible and thus understand what His will and expectations of us are.

It's not true faith to "just try our best" to do what we think pleases God. We must yield our life to Him and be molded by how He has revealed himself (Romans 12:1-2). Living faith acts on the word of God in yielding one's will to God's commandment in honor of His authority. Jesus said that the one thing <u>needful</u> is to sit at his feet (implying he's the Master whose in control) and hear his word (see Luke 10:38-42). Those who won't diligently and continually seek to understand God's truth in the Bible and act upon it regardless of personal gain/loss in this world can't exercise a living faith and thus cannot bring forth good fruit. Thus true faith cannot be separated from yielding to understand the will of God for us by how He has revealed Himself to us through Jesus Christ in the Bible (Hebrews 1:1-2). We must so yield, willing to be taught with nothing at all to hold onto. This is what Jesus meant when he said **"Verily I say unto you, Whosoever shall not receive the kingdom of God as a little child shall in no wise enter therein." (Luke 18:17)** When the Apostle Paul was first was converted to Christ his cry was **"Lord, what wilt thou have me to do?"** (see Acts 9:6)

Continuing with Luke 3:9 we look at the statement *"every tree therefore which brings not forth good fruit is hewn down, and cast into the fire."* Eternal judgment on the ungodly is a foundational truth of the gospel (Hebrews 6:2) and though popular books are written that attempt to explain it away it cannot be done without being blind to or dishonest with scripture. God will honor people's choices and will give justice by giving all exactly what is deserved by those choices. If we believe that God is immeasurably great (as He is) then the consequences of obedience or disobedience to His authority must be immeasurably great as well. It is important enough to repeat that transgressors of God's commands are not merely guilty "of doing some bad things" but of treason against the holy and righteous God of the Universe and His government. It is not merely doing bad things that people go to the fire of hell forever for, but a deep enmity against a good and perfect God which was persisted in against many chances to acknowledge and turn from that enmity, and so find mercy and life (Proverbs 29:1). It is because man would not be subject to God's authority that sin came into the world, the very thing that is the spring of all trouble, disease, sorrow, mourning, and pain that are in this world; as well as death itself.[2] Therefore all who continue to refuse to be subject to God's authority contribute in some way to the ongoing corruption of mankind and the evil in the world. That is sin's true face despite all the convenience, pleasure, and glamour that it can yield in the short-term- and why God's severity in punishing sinners is just.

The righteous punishment people deserve is what makes the mercy and love of God so deep and amazing- the gospel of Christ is God coming to rescue His very enemies who have committed treason against Him; the seriousness of which is illustrated by the dreadful just sentence hanging over their heads as well as by the agony and horror Christ went through on the cross to redeem sinners. If we sin against that amazing revelation of God's goodness as revealed in the gospel and still refuse to repent then truly there is nothing more than can be done to

---

[2]That's not to say all these things are a direct result of someone's sin necessarily. Yet all these things would not be in the world at all if sin were not in the world. This world would in that case remain a Garden Of Eden.

save us (Isaiah 5:3-4, Romans 2:4-5, Hebrews 10:26-31).

The Specific Instruction Of John

"And the people asked him, saying, What shall we do then? He answereth and saith unto them, He that hath two coats, let him impart to him that hath none; and he that hath meat (food), let him do likewise. Then came also publicans to be baptized, and said unto him, Master, what shall we do? And he said unto them, Exact no more than that which is appointed you. And the soldiers likewise demanded of him, saying, And what shall we do? And he said unto them, Do violence to no man, neither accuse any falsely; and be content with your wages." (Luke 3:10-14)

The message of John gives specific reproof and instruction to all in what one must do in order to turn to the Lord and bring forth fruits worthy of repentance according to one's situation in life, personal sinful attitudes and deeds, as well as opportunities to do good. This was in response to the people's question of what to do regarding John's authoritative declaration that every tree which brings not forth good fruit is hewn down and cast into the fire.

We should note above that in telling the people who had extra to help those who did not have enough John was NOT protesting and calling the Roman government to institute socialism. He was calling individuals to help the needy as they were able as a sign of repentance toward God by recognizing that all they have is from God and therefore must be available to help one's fellow man when he truly is in need of it- to love God with our all we must love our neighbor as ourselves, as Jesus affirmed in

Matthew 22:37-40.[3] It is a sin to EXPECT the government to provide for us when we should look to God to ultimately provide for us. We should be willing to work if we are able to do so, as God ordained that man should (when able to and not bound by other serious, pressing obligations) work for a living. Those that are able to work but are unwilling to, believing themselves entitled to handouts from others are not truly needy; and assisting them when they have this mentality is really hurting them. Same for those with addictions that they need money to support. Those that hope the government or any other person/group will solve their financial problems and put food on the table for them commit idolatry by trusting in man instead of God. Though some can legitimately receive government assistance what matters is the attitude towards it being cut off. Do we look to God or someone/something else as our ultimate provider? Likewise we are not excused from helping those who lack because we pay taxes which are used to some extent to help the needy. Even if we detect cheaters and liars there are still many opportunities that all come across or hear about to help those with a real lack in their lives which our obligations towards God make it necessary that we meet.

We see too above that John stressed total honesty in financial dealings to the publicans, the tax collectors who easily could take more than they were appointed and get away with it (in man's eyes that is). The message of John insists what Jesus also insisted on: To be right with God and be His servant we must be honest and faithful in money and not cheat anyone out of even the slightest amount in what we receive from others and in what we are

---

[3] His words in this scripture also show we can't love our neighbor as we ought without loving God first; and that true love for our neighbor must be in alignment with God's commandments.

obligated to pay to others. That means reporting all the income the laws of the nation/state we live in obligates us to report and paying all the taxes the law says we should pay. It also means paying all we owe to others and not going into debt unnecessarily; and if we are in debt that we pay off the debt as much as we are able to when we are able to do so. All the money beyond our necessities that comes through our hands if we are in debt *belongs to someone else* and we therefore don't have a right to spend it as we please (even if the creditor is a faceless bank or credit card company). The message of John insists all unrighteousness with mammon (money and possessions) and all attachment to it be ended so God can be loved and served in truth. Jesus said **"No man can serve two masters: for either he will hate the one, and love the other; or else he will hold to the one, and despise the other. Ye cannot serve God and mammon." (Matthew 6:24)** We see too in John's statement to the tax collectors that we need to be subject to God's commandments in the areas of our lives that are hidden from other people and known only to God (our thoughts and our deeds done in secret/anonymously).

We see too above that John also emphasized to the Roman soldiers present to not do violence to anyone, to accuse none falsely, and to be content with their wages.[4] Many soldiers were using their position and influence to extort money and take advantage of people. They were essentially bullies. John's call is that any power, position, privilege, or influence any may have here be used to protect and serve others and not be used for unlawful gain and/or troubling/oppressing/falsely accusing others at all. The earth being full of violence was a key aspect of its corruption in Noah's time which caused the Lord to

---

[4] A great lesson for today- contentment is the opposite of covetousness/greed- see 1 Timothy 6:6-10.

destroy the earth and nearly everyone on it by a flood (see Genesis 6:11-13). Now much television programming and many movies glorify violence, crime, and many other forms of behavior that are harmful and destructive. Shows that are filled with insults, cursing, mean-spirited debate, and malice are well-liked and popular in our society (violence of words is very destructive too and a common form of extortion and oppression now). The Bible is clear that those who take pleasure in the wickedness of others share in their guilt (see Romans 1:32). Internet chatrooms, discussion forums, and social networking sites are often likewise so used, and even more in that they are a common means of false accusation also. Rumors and accusations are often spread about people that those spreading and taking in often get excited about; which in many cases do not even have substantial evidence to prove they are even true. This is evil, along with much else that is on the internet.

In continuing with John's instruction regarding contentment with one's wages in Luke 3:10-14: It's worth noting that the anger and complaining common now, especially regarding the economy and politics, likewise shows the corruption of our society. The Bible says that murmurers and complainers are those who walk after their own lusts (and thus not the will of God) and thus the source of complaining is that their lusts are not satisfied. However those lusts will never be satisfied *on a continual basis* and thus any significant disturbance to fulfilling them as desired will result in complaining, at least at heart. **"Hell and destruction are never full; so the eyes of man are never satisfied." (Proverbs 27:20) "These are murmurers, complainers, walking after their own lusts" (Jude 16a).** The message of John insists we repent of covetousness and be content with our (lawfully received) income, possessions, financial situation, etc. That doesn't mean it's wrong to take a better job, receive a pay raise, or seek improvement of quality in other areas of life; but the issues are, "Do we become angry/fretful and start complaining if things stay the same or get worse? Do we break the law of God or man at all to get what we want?"

A great lesson in these examples is that to bring forth fruit fit for repentance we must turn from living our own way with the intent to honor God's righteous commands in everything we do- both inwardly in the thoughts and intents of our heart; as well as in our actions, words, and dealings with other people. To bring forth the fruit of repentance there must be (presently) nothing that God or man (rightfully) has a controversy with us over that we could make right but haven't- nothing we are doing (or are intent on doing) that we are forbidden to do; nor any obligation we are neglecting to do (or are intent on neglecting) which we ought to do. It's necessary also to make right whatever we can regarding our past sins and completely renounce them in order to give glory to God (Psalm 24:3-6). Not glorifying Him as God and thus not being subject to His authority and commandments is why God's wrath is revealed against mankind to begin with (see Romans 1:18-21).

Reproof Of All Evil

"But Herod the tetrarch, being reproved by him for Herodias his brother Philip's wife, and for all the evils which Herod had done, Added yet this above all, that he shut up John in prison." (Luke 3:19-20)

We learn from the passage above that the message of John reproves all evils. Jesus reiterated this reproof in John 3:18-20 by showing that refusal to completely forsake evil deeds is why people cannot come to him in faith and so avoid condemnation. This reproof and instruction is why the message of John is opposed and why John was imprisoned and eventually beheaded as we see by reading the gospels in their entirety. The world as a whole will not take Jesus on his terms, and that is why he was persecuted and why all who prepare the way for him like John and who stand for Christ's truth shall be persecuted in some way (see John 7:7, John 15:18-21, and 2 Timothy 3:12).

There are many sins that are common in America and the rest of the world (often influenced by America) which are running out of control and being embraced by multitudes. Many of those embracing these sins are professing Christians who believe themselves to be saved by faith in Jesus Christ but who scorn the authority and truth of God. The message of John the Baptist exposes the works of darkness in men and insists people leave the broad way and thus stop following the world's ways in order to follow Jesus Christ and walk in obedience to him.

Evil works which the Bible condemns such as telling lies, breaking promises/legal contracts, spite, strife, malice/ill-will, wrath, bitterness, gossip, dishonor of parents, boasting, adultery, sex outside of marriage[5], pornography and other forms of lust/immodesty, drunkenness, using drugs to get high (called sorcery in the Bible), different forms of theft, covetousness and various forms of idolatry- idolatry through loving money and seeking security in it, idolatry over politics, idolatry in <u>being consumed/taken up with</u> pleasure/sports/the internet/other technology-related entertainment, and/or other forms of leisure and entertainment, mockery and/or neglect of the less fortunate, envy/jealousy towards the rich, using God's name in vain (casually and/or in

---

[5] Marriage as defined by God in the Bible- see Jesus' words in Matthew 19:4-5.

anger/frustration) and many other sins abound in our society which also infect other nations in a great way, as America's influence towards the rest of the world is so great. Again, the issue is way more than just the evil works; it is the contempt of God in the evil works that are practiced and the good that is neglected. We have learned to be impulsive and to do and say whatever we feel like, to be driven by our own wants, and to go about life as if it is about our own pleasure. Yet God created all things for His pleasure and obedience to Him must be our primary concern in everything.

"Thou art worthy, O Lord, to receive glory and honor and power: for thou hast created all things, and for thy pleasure they are and were created." (Revelation 4:11)

"But seek ye first the kingdom of God, and his righteousness; and all these things shall be added unto you." (Matthew 6:33)

"Pure religion and undefiled before God and the Father is this, To visit the fatherless and widows in their affliction, and to keep himself unspotted from the world." (James 1:27)

Are we willing to honestly pray to God to show us how we must bring forth fruit that is fit for repentance in our own lives AND actually open our eyes and ears to receive an answer? Are we willing to read the Bible in expectation that our hearts might be seen for what they really are and that we might receive instruction on how we must get our hearts right and thus **"have a conscience void of offense toward God, and towards men." (Acts 24:16)** Will we honestly pray: **"Search me, O God, and know my heart: try me, and know my thoughts: And see if there be any wicked way in me, and lead me in** the way everlasting." (Psalm 139:23-24)?

The Supremacy of Christ And His Judgment By Fire

"And as the people were in expectation, and all men mused in their hearts of John, whether he were the Christ, or not; John answered, saying unto them all, I indeed baptize you with water; but one mightier than I cometh, the latchet of whose shoes I am not worthy to unloose: he shall baptize you with the Holy Ghost and with fire: Whose fan is in his hand, and he will throughly purge his floor, and will gather the wheat into his garner; but the chaff he will burn with fire unquenchable." (Luke 3:15-17)

The message of John recognizes the supremacy of Jesus Christ, makes it clear that he is the only true God and Savior, and that he ought to be preeminent in everything. We should heed John that we might worship Jesus in truth, and thus keep his word and no longer go our own way. The message of John prepares those who heed it to come under the reign of Jesus Christ, enter the kingdom of God[6], and be baptized with his Holy Spirit (Acts 2:38-39- this is the true New Testament salvation and what it means to be truly born again). We must through Christ be delivered from sin's dominion and led by God's Spirit which comes in the form of fire to purify the heart of the one who truly believes on Jesus so that the unquenchable fire of God's judgment on ungodliness and impurity will not come upon

---

[6]The kingdom of God is a present kingdom which we must enter and live in presently in this world in order to enter the ultimate, eternal kingdom of God in the future. We will look at what the present kingdom of God is and explain it in detail in chapter 4, as it is very important and closely related to this chapter.

them on the day of judgment. **"For our God is a consuming fire." (Hebrews 12:29)**

The message of John also emphasizes that Jesus Christ is the judge of all mankind who will come again in power and glory, whom all must stand before and judged by, and who will carry out the righteous judgment of God, both in the salvation of the righteous and the damnation of the wicked. Jesus would say **"As therefore the tares (weeds) are gathered and burned in the fire; so shall it be in the end of this world. The Son of man shall send forth his angels, and they shall gather out of his kingdom all things that offend, and them which do iniquity; And shall cast them into a furnace of fire: there shall be wailing and gnashing of teeth. Then shall the righteous shine forth as the sun in the kingdom of their Father. Who hath ears to hear, let him hear." (Matthew 13:40-43).**

The Rest Of John's Message

"And many other things in his exhortation preached he unto the people." (Luke 3:18)

We don't know exactly everything else John said in his exhortation to the people. We have recorded that which we need though. We have a hint at some of the rest of what John preached by the prophecy regarding John the Baptist in Isaiah 40. After Isaiah 40:3-5 which was quoted directly in Luke 3:4-6 earlier, we are told more about John's cry in the wilderness.

"The voice said, Cry. And he said, What shall I cry? All flesh is grass, and all the goodliness thereof is as the flower of the field: The grass withers, the flower fades: because the spirit of the Lord blows upon it: surely the people is grass. The grass withers, the flower fades:

but the word of our God shall stand for ever." (Isaiah 40:6-8)

The frailty/uncertainty of life, and certain death of all- even the richest, strongest, most attractive, most athletic, and most talented in other ways is all the more reason to heed everything that has been said up until now in John's message. Who were the great athletes, the richest, strongest, most famous, most attractive, most successful people of the 1950s? You'd have to have an above average knowledge of history to know more than one or two in each category. Where are those now that had what the world most admires and strives for? Either really old or dead. Just a 60 year span has destroyed virtually all the glory of mankind from the 1950s. Any trace remaining will soon be gone. It's worth noting that it's inevitable all of man's current and future glory will also fade away and be forgotten. The word of God nevertheless stands and all yet face eternal consequences over their response in their lifetime to the word of God. So much of what we busy ourselves with and set our affections on will brought to dust and be irrelevant forever. The pleasures of life will end, as well as the sufferings of those who have done God's will. Our response to God's word will yield glory or shame which will remain forever. When Christ returns it is certain that **"the loftiness of man shall be bowed down, and the haughtiness of men shall be made low: and the Lord alone shall be exalted in that day." (Isaiah 2:17)**

"Love not the world, neither the things that are in the world. If any man love the world, the love of the Father is not in him. For all that is in the world, the lust of the flesh, and the lust of the eyes, and the pride of life, is not of the Father, but is of the world. And the world passes away, and the lust thereof: but he that does the will of God abides for ever." (1 John 2:15-17)

What reason then to sober up regarding the widespread drunkenness over the cares of this life and prepare for eternity that we might have an eternal hope and not be ashamed at Christ's coming. Now we'll focus on the event that is central to Jesus' life and ministry, without which there could be no salvation and hope for anyone. The purpose of this event and the true identity of Jesus is also borne witness to by John the Baptist.

"The next day John sees Jesus coming unto him, and saith, Behold the Lamb of God, which taketh away the sin of the world... And I saw, and bare record that this is the Son of God." (John 1:29, 34)

Chapter 3:
Christ Has Made A Way Through The Cross

The just penalty for sinning against God is death. A death beyond physical death to the body which is ultimate and true death, the cutting off of one's soul from God, the source of all life and light. This was the death Adam and Eve died when they ate the fruit of the tree. God had guaranteed in Genesis 2:17 that this would surely occur should they so eat of the tree. So all who have transgressed and disobeyed the Lord have likewise died. Being dead in sin means that the life-giving relationship with the Father has been cut off; it doesn't however make a person on this earth totally unable to perceive truth and hear the voice of God. We see God speaking to and dealing with Adam and Eve in Genesis 3 right after they died spiritually. Nevertheless they had sold themselves to sin's slavery and were thus cut off from a living union with the Living God; and all who have followed them in transgressing the Lord are thus doomed to being so cut off both here and in eternity- unless a way were to be made to restore that union. We are looking now at what God has done to restore that union that we might yet be made alive.

The significance of a blood sacrifice in the Bible is a key theme. There is no remission of sins and reconciliation with the Lord without the shedding of blood (Hebrews 9:22). Though animal blood cannot of itself take away sins, it was by God's commandment shed constantly in the Old Testament when a person sinned as a lesson that sin is extremely costly and cannot be taken away if there is not a life offered up as a sacrifice in the place of the sinner. It is more than just the physical life that is the issue. It is the issue of the atonement of the soul, an entire being yielded and offered up to God in place of the one who should justly die. For God to be just and His absolute holiness to be honored there must be a soul (an entire being), a perfect life with no sin of its own to pay for, given as a ransom when one sins against the Lord in order to make an atonement for the sinner's soul so that the sinner may be reconciled to Him and their soul (entire being) not cast away eternally.[7]

The most fearful, sobering, amazing act of human history was when the price was paid for the way of salvation to be opened. In this the just, holy wrath of God against sinners and the love of God towards His sinful, fallen creation would be demonstrated in one day in a shocking way. This is what happened at the cross when both the love of God toward sinners and the holy hatred of God towards sin were demonstrated in the central event of human history; when Christ, the spotless lamb of God, bore the sin of the world in his body and offered up his soul as an offering to God so those dead in sin could be pardoned and made alive again.

Christ had To Overcome Temptation As A Man

For this to happen though he could not merely show up as an adult one day and die and all be

---

[7]See Leviticus 17:11 regarding the OT lesson of how God proved the need for a blood sacrifice to make atonement for the soul; and Leviticus 22:21-24 on how that atonement had to be made through no less than a perfect sacrifice.

accomplished. He had to be that truly perfect life that could in truth be offered without spot to God as a ransom for the guilty. For though Jesus was perfect from the day he was born he actually had to overcome every (type of) temptation people face in order to be the perfect sacrifice. That is how we can understand this scripture:

"Who in the days of his flesh, when he had offered up prayers and supplications with strong crying and tears unto him that was able to save him from death, and was heard in that he feared; Though he were a Son, yet learned he obedience by the things which he suffered; And being made perfect, he became the author of eternal salvation unto all them that obey him" (Hebrews 5:7-9)

This overcoming was necessary in order for him to sympathize with us and to help us overcome temptation as well. As the previous scripture shows, Christ died for us that we might follow him in obedience and overcome by him as well. Christ's life was also necessary to testify of God's true character to us and to demonstrate and proclaim the full truth about God to mankind. **"No man hath seen God at any time, the only begotten Son, which is in the bosom of the Father, he hath declared him." (John 1:18)**

Jesus' life then was in a sense a death from start to finish- a death to self. He is the true God who humbled himself and forsook his own convenience in heaven and his rights he could have claimed as God (even though did not cease to be God when he lived as a man). He chose the lowest birthplace in a stable, he had a lowly upbringing, was subject to authorities that he could have claimed a right to rule over, and did not exercise his power as God when it came to fulfilling his own needs and wants. He really lived as a man and experienced what people experience- without sin. He did not refrain from sin because the temptation was not there. When the devil tempted him in the wilderness, the scripture is not lying when it says he was tempted of the devil (Matthew 4:1). He really was hungry after fasting 40 days, he really was tempted to misuse his authority to turn stones into bread, he really was tempted to take the easy road and be exalted without doing the Father's will and going to the cross. So his whole life he yielded up his rights as God and lived as a man by faith in His Father as Adam should have lived, not only in one trial, but in multiple trials and every sort of trial- all to lift us out of the condition of spiritual death and restore us to union with the Father.

Christ's life on earth was also necessary for him to be the head of a new race after his death and resurrection- not a physical race, but a spiritual race of people from all natural races and ethnicities who are redeemed from sin and transferred out of Adam's race to be alive to the will of God; opposed to being dead in sin and enslaved to their own desires like Adam's race is characterized by (Ephesians 2:2-3). This is a key truth in God's ultimate purpose in His dealings with mankind. Hence Jesus is called **"the last Adam"** (in 1 Corinthians 15:45) and the New Testament from the beginning is said to be **"The book of the generation of Jesus Christ, the son of David, the son of Abraham" (Matthew 1:1)**

Christ's Great Humility Shown By His Great Worth

Jesus' life was the essence of true love, or as the King James Version says, of charity, which is exemplified completely in him. **"Charity suffers long** (is patient)**, and is kind; charity envies not; charity vaunts not** (boasts not) **itself, is not puffed up, Doth not behave itself unseemly** (indecent, shameful, inappropriate)**, seeks**

not her own, is not easily provoked, thinks no evil; Rejoices not in iniquity, but rejoices in the truth; Bears all things, believes all things[8], hopes all things[9], endures all things." (1 Corinthians 13:4-7)

The Bible thus describes Christ's humility, his constant death to his own will, which is how/why he walked in charity. **"Who, being in the form of God, thought it not robbery to be equal with God: But made himself of no reputation, and took upon him the form of a servant, and was made in the likeness of men: And being found in fashion as a man, he humbled himself, and became obedient unto death, even the death of the cross." (Philippians 2:6-8)**

I heard a certain preacher say how when he speaks at universities he just loves hearing the question that university students often ask "How can one man pay the penalty for the sins of billions of people?" He loves the question because he loves to give the answer *"Because this life is worth more than all the others combined!"*

So as Jesus came to the end of his earthly life he knew it was time that he offer himself up to God finally to be the perfect sacrifice and spotless soul offered to God as a ransom for the guilty. He went off alone in the Garden of Gethsemane and prayed **"O my Father, if it be possible, let this cup pass from me: nevertheless not as I will, but as thou wilt." (Matthew 26:39b)** We see shortly after how Jesus surrendered to this fearful duty of drinking **"this cup."** **"He went away again the second time, and prayed, saying, O my Father, if this cup may**

---

[8]Believes all things God has spoken; believes the best about others until given proof otherwise.

[9]Hopes in every promise God has made and therefore does not despair; hopes for the best for others.

not pass away from me, except I drink it, thy will be done." (Matthew 26:42) We learn from the events that followed that there really was no other possible way for sin to be atoned for but by Jesus going to the cross. But what was the cup Jesus spoke of?

The Cup Christ Drank

It was far more than just the wrath of man which Christ suffered- more than the hatred of the Jews, the mockery of the Romans, the whip, and the nails whereby he was fastened to the cross. *It was* the torment of the soul as he experienced the wrath due to sinners as it fell upon him, the sinless one, as he took the place of the guilty. There is a sense in which Barabbas, the notorious criminal, whom the Roman Governor Pilate released instead of Christ, is a picture of mankind. **"For Christ also hath once suffered for sins, the just for the unjust, that he might bring us to God, being put to death in the flesh, but quickened by the Spirit." (1 Peter 3:18)** The weight of our sins was laid on Christ as he bore them on the cross. **"Surely he hath borne our griefs, and carried our sorrows: yet we did esteem him stricken, smitten of God, and afflicted. But he was wounded for our transgressions, he was bruised for our iniquities: the chastisement of our peace was upon him; and with his stripes we are healed. All we like sheep have gone astray; we have turned every one to his own way; and the Lord hath laid on him the iniquity of us all." (Isaiah 53:4-6)**

The cup of the Lord is described in the Bible as the cup of God's anger and fury. God spoke in the Old Testament about the cup of His judgment that the wicked must drink from His hand (see for example Psalm 75:8 and Jeremiah 25:28-29). This is what Christ bore on the cross and it was awful!

We see glimpses into the anguish Christ suffered on the cross in drinking this cup from prophecies of him in the Book of Psalms, which Jesus spoke of as repeatedly testifying of him, as well as the rest of the Old Testament (Luke 24:44). **"Thou hast laid me in the lowest pit, in darkness, in the deeps. Thy wrath lies hard upon me, and thou hast afflicted me with all thy waves... Thou hast put away mine acquaintance far from me; thou hast made me an abomination unto them: I am shut up, and I cannot come forth." (Psalm 88:6-8)** In the sufferings of Abel, Joseph, Job, Moses, Jeremiah, Daniel, and in many of God's other servants in the Bible we see pictures of Christ, the righteous man suffering in place of the guilty and for the sake of the guilty. The cup of God's wrath is the cup of true death which Christ drank in full on the cross. **"But we see Jesus, who was made a little lower than the angels for the suffering of death, crowned with glory and honor; that he by the grace of God should taste death for every man." (Hebrews 2:9)**

The Victory Of The Cross

Christ suffered as a man, for only a man can die for men. He yet did not cease to be God and as he offered himself up through the eternal Spirit (Hebrews 9:14) he could thus pay an infinite penalty, his suffering being of eternal worth and his life of greater value of all others, both inherently and actually by virtue of his completely holy and righteous life. His soul, represented by his blood, was given as an atonement to (potentially) redeem us out of death back into union with our Creator.

"For the life of the flesh is in the blood: and I have given it to you upon the altar to make an atonement for your souls: for it is the blood that makes an atonement for the soul." (Leviticus 17:11)

"Yet it pleased the Lord to bruise him; he hath put him to grief: when thou shalt make his soul an offering for sin, he shall see his seed, he shall prolong his days, and the pleasure of the Lord shall prosper in his hand." (Isaiah 53:10)

Jesus could rightfully say **"It is finished" (John 19:30)** as his body died. The ransom price had been paid and the way to life was opened by Christ's faithfulness and sacrifice. His soul had been poured out fully and his precious blood had made the atonement. Now there is a way of salvation and now the Father would honor His Son by exalting him- proving he is truly the one who is the Son of God and that his sacrifice is indeed accepted by the Father.

The Nature Of Sin Displayed By The Cross

We also see at the cross the true nature of sin being displayed. We see that those who transgress God at heart actually commit treason against Him and pour out bitter hatred against His holy and righteous government. This is that contempt of God already spoken of in chapter 2 that is the real reason people go to hell beyond the acts of sin in and of themselves. The cross was when the Father allowed that bitter enmity of people against Him to be demonstrated in reality upon His Son as he was made a curse upon it as the sins of the world were laid upon him (Galatians 3:13); and thus made sin to be seen for what it is in its essence. That is why when Jesus was arrested he told his enemies **"This is your hour, and the power of darkness." (Luke 22:53b)** Of course those who actually crucified Jesus were unaware God's intention in allowing this, as were the devil and his forces (1 Corinthians 2:8). God overruled the greatest evil of people and of Satan (Acts 2:23) to bring about the greatest possible good for people as well as the defeat of Satan (Hebrews 2:14-15).

This was all allowed for the (potential) benefit of sinners, God's very enemies!

The Importance Of The Kingdom Of God In Relation To Who Christ Is And What He Has Done

We will see in the next chapter how Jesus died and rose again to establish the kingdom of God; and how receiving that kingdom is the condition to being restored to God through Christ and brought out of spiritual death through his death and resurrection. The message of John the Baptist is essential in that when it is heeded it prepares us to receive Christ's kingdom- and so partake of the atonement he purchased for us on the cross and have access to his saving, transforming power he makes available as he now sits in heaven to be the one mediator between God and men (1 Timothy 2:5). Understanding the kingdom of God and responding rightly to it is a matter of eternal life or death, as it is tied inseparably to the purpose of the gospel of Christ and thus how we are obligated to respond to Christ if we are to be saved through his gospel. Rightly understanding the kingdom of God is essential to understanding the significance of Christ's coming to earth, his atonement on the cross, his resurrection and position now, the ultimate message of the Bible, and thus even God's ultimate purpose for mankind. In the next chapter then we will look at the kingdom of God in detail and seek to explain what it means for us today in light of what we have looked at already; and what it will mean to all in the future based on our present response to the kingdom here and now.

Chapter 4:
Being In Christ Means Being In The Kingdom Of God

The Resurrection- The Father Bearing Witness To Christ

The end of Jesus' life of obedience and offering his soul to God was the Father raising him from the dead by the power of the Holy Spirit and crowning him Lord of all, not only by his right as Christ the Son of God, but by his purchase of people from the bondage of sin by pouring out his soul unto death. Though men rejected Christ, the resurrection is God's witness of His acceptance of him and demonstration that he is indeed the Son of God and Lord of all.

"And declared to be the Son of God with power, according to the spirit of holiness, by the resurrection from the dead: By whom we have received grace and apostleship, for obedience to the faith among all nations, for his name" (Romans 1:4-5)

"Wherefore God also hath highly exalted him, and given him a name which is above every name: That at the name of Jesus every knee should bow, of things in heaven, and things in earth, and things under the earth; And that every tongue should confess that Jesus Christ is Lord, to the glory of God the Father."

(Philippians 2:9-11)

Now that the way to life has been made and our salvation prepared means that everything that sin has ruined in us can be healed (1 John 3:8). Christ was separated from the Father that we might be united to the Father through Christ. He was bruised that we might be healed. He was treated as guilty that we might be accounted innocent in him. God was turned against him that He might on our side if we are in Christ. The key now for us is to be joined to Christ by believing in him <u>in the way the Bible says we must</u>. John the Baptist also said near the end of his ministry. **"The Father loves the Son, and hath given all things into his hand. He that believes on the Son hath everlasting life: and he that believes not the Son shall not see life; but the wrath of God abides on him." (John 3:35-36)** Being raised from the bondage and death of sin into a union with the Father through Christ is true life.

The Clear Call Of The Gospel

In understanding the call of the gospel and the way to life it must be made clear that Christ did not come to die for us in order to excuse us from walking in obedience to the truth of God. Rather he came to redeem us from sin's dominion and bring us back into a living union with God that we might be enabled to. He died to destroy sin's power and rose again to enable those who believe on him to walk in true righteousness by his resurrection life in them.

"But now once in the end of the world hath he appeared to put away sin by the sacrifice of himself" (Hebrews 9:26b)

"Who his own self bare our sins in his own

body on the tree, that we being dead to sins, should live unto righteousness" (1 Peter 2:24a)

However there are false gospels out there which take what we have seen of the love of God in the sacrifice of Christ and attempt to make the good news palatable to people who don't really want to leave sin's prison because they find it pleasurable to remain and/or too bothersome to come out. Though not really good news, these false gospels seem like good news to those who don't want their way of life challenged. These false gospels say[10] that we can be saved from God's wrath even if we don't turn from sin and subject ourselves to Christ's authority and thus to his commandments. Others emphasize external actions which are given in essence is a substitute for obedience to Christ. They certainly don't preach the message of John the Baptist as the beginning of the gospel that is the necessary preparation for Christ. Being "in Christ" is the equivalent of being joined to him by saving faith and we need to see what the Bible means by that.

Jesus is our Noah[11] who has prepared the way of salvation by his own labor and expense; he calls us into that ark he has prepared away from the rebellion and sin of the world so when the wrath of God is poured out on the ungodly, disobedient world those who are in him will be spared. **"Who gave himself for our sins, that he might deliver us from this present evil world, according to the will of God and our Father: To whom be glory for ever and ever. Amen." (Galatians 1:4-5)**

The true love of God is that which seeks to save us from that which His wrath is against and our being united

---

[10] Usually not directly, but by implication.

[11] Genesis chapters 6-9 in the Old Testament contain the account of Noah's ark and the flood which we are referring to here.

to God through Christ can only be as we are agreed with Him and hate the sin which His wrath is against. Hence the need to heed the message of repentance of John the Baptist, which Jesus ordained should yet accompany his gospel. **"Thus it is written, and thus it behooved Christ to suffer, and to rise from the dead the third day: And that <u>repentance and remission of sins</u> should be preached in his name among all nations, beginning at Jerusalem." (Luke 24:46-47)**

Jesus' Reign As King Must Be Received

Jesus is a King[12] and a Savior.[13] He is a King who sets those under his reign free from their enemies.[14] <u>In order to have faith in Christ we must receive in all his offices or not truly believe in him</u>. We must yield to his reign as King, seeking for him to actually save us from the sinful way of life and sinful deeds which he died to put away. It is common for one person to ask another "Will you receive Jesus as your Savior?" Yet we can't receive Jesus as Savior and neglect him as King/Lord. At Jesus' birth the angels of God said of him **"For unto you is born this day in the city of David a Saviour, which is Christ the Lord." (Luke 2:11)** Nor can we make receiving Jesus a formality where we just say yes to the right questions. We must actually deal with the pride of our hearts that opposes Christ and causes us to go our own way so we can truly meet the necessary condition to be on his side and to

---

[12] Or we can say Lord. The New Testament uses both these words to describe Jesus' ultimate, rightful authority.

[13] We can also say he's a Prophet- as a King he enforces what he spoke as a Prophet; he is also the Great High Priest who applies what he purchased as a Savior to those who come to God by him (Hebrews 7:25).

[14] Our soul's ultimate enemies are carnal desires which result in sin when yielded to- 1 Peter 2:11.

genuinely know HIM. Thus as Jesus prayed to his Father for his disciples the night before he was crucified he said **"And this is life eternal, that they might know thee the only true God, and Jesus Christ, whom thou hast sent." (John 17:3)**

The true gospel message then is the message of the gospel of the kingdom of God- the rule and reign of God among men. God's reclaiming of His rightful authority over people.[15] We are talking now about God's present kingdom whose subjects presently bow to God's authority and are received into a life-giving union with God through the atonement and mediation of Jesus Christ, the King and Deliverer of his subjects. There is a future aspect of the kingdom of God which those who are under God's authority through Christ in the present will inherit at Christ's second coming (Romans 8:17, 1 Corinthians 15:24-28).

This message, the gospel of the kingdom of God, is the message which Jesus preached from the very beginning of his ministry as being near at hand- and continued to be preached by the Apostles as a present reality after his death and resurrection- and is still the gospel message today! We can be right with God now no

---

[15] Not a current political entity as Jesus' kingdom is now not of this world- John 18:36. Those who would be part of Jesus' kingdom must recognize and honor those in position in earthly governments as Jesus himself did; and must obey government laws and pay mandated taxes and customs. See Matthew 22:21, Romans 13:1-8 and 1 Peter 2:12-17. Romans 13:1-2 show clearly that those who resist earthly government oppose God Himself who appointed them in His sovereign wisdom. Only when a government's laws and directions conflict with God's commandments must they be disobeyed- and even then as respectfully as possible and only in the area(s) where the conflict is (see Acts 4:18-20 and 5:27-29).

matter how badly we've sinned and how unworthy we are. The condition is that we subject ourselves to His authority as God through his Son Jesus Christ and thus continue in subjection to His authority. People commit sin because they choose to go their own way rather than God's way. To receive the benefit of pardon by Christ's death and his ability to make us new and heal our sin-sick souls by his resurrection power, we have an obligation to honor his authority and turn to him to reign over us as we ought to have in the first place. We can only be found and no longer lost when we return to the place and position which, by leaving, caused us to be lost to begin with. To expect forgiveness otherwise is like the man who expects his wife to take him back though he continues in adultery!

The Kingdom Of God Can't Be Separated From The Gospel

So we see the proclamation of the kingdom of God as being hand-in-hand and consistent time after time with the gospel proclamation in the New Testament as it unfolds. We saw earlier the essential message of repentance which John the Baptist preached to prepare the way for Christ. That message was in itself a preparation for the kingdom of God, which in John the Baptist's and Jesus' days of public preaching (before Jesus' death and resurrection) was **"at hand"** as something very near but not yet arrived. In one scripture we didn't look at earlier we see that John preached the kingdom of heaven[16] with his message of repentance. **"In those days came John the Baptist, preaching in the wilderness of Judaea, And saying, Repent ye: for the kingdom of heaven is at hand." (Matthew 3:1-2)**

---

[16] Same as the kingdom of God- see Matthew 19:23-24 where the kingdom of heaven and the kingdom of God are clearly equated by Jesus.

We see then how Jesus reiterated this message in his preaching (as we said before that John the Baptist's message was reiterated by Jesus and the Apostles). **"Now after that John was put in prison, Jesus came into Galilee, preaching the gospel of the kingdom of God, And saying, The time is fulfilled, and the kingdom of God is at hand: repent ye, and believe the gospel." (Mark 1:14-15)**

The gospel of the kingdom was also the message that the Apostles and early Christians preached throughout the Book of Acts, to all people, Jews and Gentiles[17] except they preached the kingdom of God as a present reality that could be entered into immediately since Jesus had now died and rose again and sent the Holy Spirit. **"But when they believed Philip preaching the things concerning the kingdom of God, and the name of Jesus Christ, they were baptized, both men and women." (Acts 8:12)** **"And he** (Paul the Apostle) **went into the synagogue, and spake boldly for the space of three months, disputing and persuading the things concerning the kingdom of God." (Acts 19:8)** And as the Book of the Acts of the Apostles closes we are told: **"And Paul dwelt two whole years in his own hired house, and received all that came in unto him, Preaching the kingdom of God, and teaching those things which concern the Lord Jesus Christ, with all confidence, no man forbidding him." (Acts 28:31)**

Looking At A Critical Truth

It is a critical truth to see that the Bible shows receiving forgiveness of sins as together with being

---

[17] That is a key truth, the gospel of the kingdom of God is the gospel message for everyone.

delivered from Satan's kingdom and power over unto God's kingdom and power. Thus Paul wrote of God's deliverance of himself and all those genuinely in Christ. **"Who hath delivered us from the power of darkness, and hath translated us into the kingdom of his dear Son: in whom we have redemption through his blood, even the forgiveness of sins (Colossians 1:13-14)**

A change of direction in turning to God in repentance in order to believe on Christ and thus receiving this deliverance of God through Christ must occur at a given point (for all like sheep have gone astray- Isaiah 53:6); and then be walked in and continued in from there. That is what it means to live in the present kingdom of God. **"As ye have therefore received Christ Jesus the Lord, so walk ye in him: Rooted and built up in him, and established in the faith, as ye have been taught, abounding therein with thanksgiving." (Colossians 2:6-7)**

There are only two alternatives for us with nothing in between: To be under the reign of sin/Satan or to be under the reign of Christ as his disciple in the kingdom of God. Jesus said **"He that is not with me is against me; and he that gathers not with me scatters abroad." (Matthew 12:30) "Then said Jesus to those Jews which believed on him, If ye continue in my word, then are ye my disciples indeed; And ye shall know the truth, and the truth shall make you free. They answered him, We be Abraham's seed, and were never in bondage to any man: how sayest thou, Ye shall be made free? Jesus answered them, Verily, verily, I say unto you, Whosoever commits sin is the servant of sin. And the servant abides not in the house for ever: but the Son abides ever. If the Son therefore shall make you free, ye shall be free indeed." (John 8:31-36)**

So to be in the kingdom of God is to be under the authority of God through Jesus the King of mankind and be subject to his righteous reign- for he died and rose again in order to be our Lord (see Romans 14:9).

Genuine Obedience To Jesus Defines His Kingdom

Jesus' kingdom is based upon the truth of God and being a subject in his kingdom is characterized by siding with Jesus in loving righteousness and hating iniquity (transgression of God's commandments) <u>as defined by the truth of God's word</u>.[18] **"But unto the Son he saith, Thy throne, O God, is for ever and ever: a scepter[19] of righteousness is the scepter of thy kingdom. Thou hast loved righteousness, and hated iniquity; therefore God, even thy God, hath anointed thee with the oil of gladness above thy fellows." (Hebrews 1:8-9)** We see by Jesus' words to Pilate on the day he was crucified that in this present age before his second coming his kingdom is not in competition with present earthly rulers but is based upon the truth of God being obeyed in those who heed his voice, those who receive him as their King/Lord and are therefore ruled by his words. **"Jesus answered, My kingdom is not of this world: if my kingdom were of this world, then would my servants fight, that I should not be delivered to the Jews: but now is my kingdom not from hence. Pilate therefore said unto him, Art thou a king then? Jesus answered, <u>Thou sayest that I am a king. To this end was I born, and for this cause</u>**

---

[18]The ultimate difference between eating of the tree of knowledge of good and evil and thus rebelling against God's authority versus having access to the tree of life comes down to the issue of whether we attempt to decide right and wrong for ourselves or look to God through Christ to teach us through an obedient relationship in honor of His authority.

[19]A rod-like instrument which represents royal authority.

came I into the world, that I should bear witness unto the truth. Every one that is of the truth hears my voice." (John 18:36-37)

Jesus is the full revelation of God's character, and the ultimate Authority/Leader/Master[20] who knows wrong from right and has fully lived according to God's truth. He is the light of God whereby God has demonstrated the true righteousness of His commandments who calls us to follow him in obedient faith. We are expected therefore to come to the light and walk in it- and therefore hear his word and keep it. What we have in the gospels is Jesus explaining, clarifying, and applying the universal law of God by his example and instruction. We also have in the rest of the New Testament instruction on the New Covenant in Christ which we must relate to God by on the terms thereof; as well as further application of living out Jesus' commandments through his Apostles. His word is in agreement too with the moral principles of the law[21] given by Moses and the words God spoke through the Old

---

[20] See Hebrews 1:1-3

[21] No doubt there are certain aspects of the Old Testament law which are not obligations for us now, as they deal with things like sacrifices for sin, priesthood, and Temple service which have now been fulfilled in Christ; and there are issues relating to earthly/civil government which were given to Israel as a political nation which are not for the New Covenant as Christ's kingdom is not now of this world as a political entity. However the moral principles of God never change since God's character never changes; and Jesus in the gospels reproved sin by the diagnosis of Moses' law. The Sermon on the Mount in Matthew chapters 5-7 is Jesus magnifying and honoring the moral law proclaimed in the OT, and explaining the true keeping of God's commandments from the heart as opposed to the mere external conformity taught by the religious leaders of his time; which was (and is) used by lawless people as an attempt to excuse sin as they sought "loopholes" to break God's commandments.

Testament prophets (see Matthew 7:12).

The essential aspect of being subject to Jesus and keeping his words is that of the cross. We can never die to atone for the sins of the world like Jesus did on his cross- yet Jesus calls us to take up our cross to find the life he died on the cross to give us. Many think of "our crosses" as our problems in life- but Jesus spoke of the cross in the sense of dying to selfish ambition and desires to keep his word. Taking up the cross is necessary to honor his authority as God and thereby obey the gospel of the kingdom and know true life. **"And when he had called the people unto him with his disciples also, he said unto them, Whosoever will come after me, let him deny himself, and take up his cross, and follow me. For whosoever will save his life shall lose it; but whosoever shall lose his life for my sake and the gospel's, the same shall save it." (Mark 8:34-35)** Whether we take up the cross or not shows who the ultimate authority in our life is. Do I rule myself or does Christ? If he does, then his word is final and must be sought and obeyed whatever the earthly consequences of doing so. Death to self-will is the universal condition of receiving life from God. This condition is the significance of the flaming sword the Lord placed to guard the tree of life after Adam and Eve were banished from the the garden (Genesis 3:24).

Another way to understand the cross is Jesus' summary of the greatest commandments in the law of God. **"Jesus said unto him, Thou shalt love the Lord thy God with all thy heart, and with all thy soul, and with all thy mind. This is the first and great commandment. And the second is like unto it, Thou shalt love thy neighbor as thyself. On these two commandments hang all the law and the prophets." (Matthew 22:37-40)**

To love God with all one's heart necessarily means seeking what is acceptable or not acceptable to God in all things and not leaning on your understanding[22], it means self is denied when self-interest/desire and God's commandments are in conflict; it means the Lord reigns in one's heart with no rivals to Him[23]; as well as meaning that natural desires are denied in order to do to others as we would have them to do unto us.[24]

The message of John the Baptist is so important in relation to Jesus' kingdom, as John's message exposes works of darkness in accordance with the entire word of God and insists that we utterly repent and forsake them in order to come to Christ the true light and receive him for who he is. If we could just "accept Jesus as our Savior" without bowing to his rule and reign the message of John the Baptist would be a deception! It may be good at this point to go back and read, or at least recall, the first two chapters of this book since they are directly tied together with what's being said here and deal so plainly with the obstacles all face regarding being a partaker of Christ's

---

[22] See Proverbs 3:5-8

[23] See the accounts of the Rich young ruler in Matthew 19:16-30, Mark 10:17-31, and Luke 18:18-30 which illustrate this and other closely related truths. Jesus knew the man's heart and saw that it needed to be torn from the love of money and earthly things in order for him to take up the cross, follow Jesus, and have eternal life.

[24] The story of the Good Samaritan in Luke 10:25-37 is an example from Jesus of what it means to love your neighbor as yourself. We can see there the labor and expense the Samaritan went through in order to see that the wounded man was cared for properly. He had to deny his own natural desires for an easy trip, his natural desire to not lose time and to keep his plans intact, his natural desire to spend his money on himself/his family, his natural desire to not help one who may very well not have helped him if he were such a case, as well as deny himself in other ways- in order to truly love his neighbor as himself.

kingdom. Jesus himself endorsed John the Baptist's ministry (Matthew 11:7-19) and his own words testify **"He that believes on him**[25] **is not condemned: but he that believes not is condemned already, because he hath not believed in the name of the only begotten Son of God. And this is the condemnation, that light is come into the world, and men loved darkness rather than light, because their deeds were evil. For every one that does evil hates the light, neither cometh to the light, lest his deeds should be reproved." (John 3:18-20)**

Jesus' Great And Awesome Authority

Thus to receive Jesus we must turn to walk in his way and therefore must seek to obey all he commanded or we despise his kingly authority. Many go to the Bible, particularly the gospels, to get advice for life; but to take it as that alone is a great error. A royal proclamation from a wise King is certainly good advice, but if it's not taken as an obligation to be received in its entirety then it shows dishonor to the King's authority.

Jesus thus said to his disciples after his resurrection **"All power is given unto me in heaven and in earth. Go ye therefore, and teach all nations, baptizing them in the name of the Father, and of the Son, and of the Holy Ghost: Teaching them to observe all things whatsoever I have commanded you: and, lo, I am with you always, even unto the end of the world." (Matthew 28:18b-20)** That Jesus must be received as Lord and truly obeyed is the Apostolic gospel message, as we see from the conclusion of the gospel message that the Apostle Peter gave on the day of Pentecost in his instruction to his hearers on how to be made right with God. **"Therefore let all the house of Israel know**

---

[25] Jesus is referring to himself here in the third-person.

assuredly, that God hath made the same Jesus, whom ye have crucified, both Lord and Christ. Now when they heard this, they were pricked in their heart, and said unto Peter and to the rest of the apostles, Men and brethren, what shall we do? Then Peter said unto them, Repent, and be baptized every one of you in the name of Jesus Christ for the remission of sins, and ye shall receive the gift of the Holy Ghost. For the promise is unto you, and to your children, and to all that are afar off, even as many as the Lord our God shall call. And with many other words did he testify and exhort, saying, Save yourselves from this untoward (wayward) **generation." (Acts 2:36-40)**

We see from the scriptures we just looked at from Matthew chapter 28 and Acts chapter 2 that Jesus gave a basic, foundational command to be baptized as a demonstration of repentance and a new life as his disciple where he is the Master/King. It is not the act of getting baptized in itself or the water of baptism that save; but the heart that is subject to Christ and because of that subjection obeys his command to be baptized. One who has believed on Jesus with a truly obedient heart will obey his command to be baptized[26] when they are aware of it out of a good conscience towards God (1 Peter 3:21), whereas the one who neglects it or any other commandment for New Testament Christians proves their contempt of Jesus' commandments and thus of his authority. One whose heart is truly obedient to Christ who doesn't understand the command of baptism or really hasn't had a chance to carry it out will still be saved as long as they are walking in the light they do have and are seeking God in humility for more understanding of how He wills to be worshipped and served. Here we can

---

[26] The Bible knows of no true baptism but that which is done out of obedient faith.

understand Jesus' words: **"And he said unto them, Go ye into all the world, and preach the gospel to every creature. He that believes and is baptized shall be saved; but he that believes not shall be damned." (Mark 16:15-16)** Those who say they believe he's God but don't hear and/or obey him don't truly believe in him in the way the Bible says we must- as well as those who consider Jesus a great man and/or admire his character and good works/miracles yet don't receive his reign over them as God.

Contrary to the modern way Jesus is portrayed in the media he was certainly not an effeminate man with long hair. That typical image of Jesus now is a false jesus meant to appeal to the crowd of the western world and is completely made up by minds not influenced by the word of God at all. We don't know exactly how Jesus really looked when he was a man on earth, nor do we need to; but we can conclude he looked like a typical first-century Jewish man. In scriptures like Mark 14:43-46 and the other gospel accounts of Jesus' arrest we can see that the Jewish authorities needed Judas to point out Jesus to them among his disciples, though they had seen him before. It's reasonable to conclude that Jesus couldn't have stood out much in a crowd of first-century Jewish men, among whom the modern false jesus would indeed have stood out greatly! This is an important matter to address because we tend to think of men in the Old Testament like Moses and Elijah as these rugged, authoritative men while thinking of Jesus as this timid, weak acting guy. However Jesus spoke with even more authority than Moses and Elijah and every other man of God in the Bible. Jesus' authority is actually why the people were most amazed by his message! (see Matthew 7:28-29, Luke 4:36, John 7:44-46, etc) Scrap the modern image of Jesus from your mind. It is a misleading, shallow, counterfeit of the real Jesus.

Jesus was humble and gentle no doubt, but we need to define those words according to the Bible and not by modern concepts of them. Moses was called the most humble man on earth of his time (see Numbers 12:3). If Moses could speak with great authority and yet be humble no doubt Jesus could have, and did, greatly exceed Moses in both! The key is that Jesus was silent and showed meekness when it came to things like defending himself from false accusation yet he was fearfully aggressive when it came to defending his Father's honor and confronting the corruption of God's worship. Those who read the account in John 2:13-17 of one of the times Jesus drove out those selling merchandise in the Temple which was supposed to be set apart for God's worship will see that very well! **"He that despised Moses' law died without mercy under two or three witnesses: Of how much sorer punishment, suppose ye, shall he be thought worthy, who hath trodden under foot the Son of God..." (Hebrews 10:28-29a) "See that ye refuse not him that speaks. For if they escaped not who refused him that spake on earth** (referring to Moses)**, much more shall not we escape, if we turn away from him that speaks from heaven** (referring to Christ).**" (Hebrews 12:25)**

To separate faith in Jesus Christ at all from a life subject to his awesome kingly authority where he is really followed as God is a grave error. Since he is God he must be actually be followed as God. Hopefully nobody would say that someone who worships a god of wood or stone is a saved Christian. Yet one who doesn't worship Jesus and thus obey his commands from the heart even though he makes a profession of faith and salvation in him is absolutely no different than one who bows to a god of wood or stone! Like the people in Elijah's time, so now many want to find a middle ground where Jesus can somehow worshipped as God but not actually followed wholeheartedly in obedience. Yet there is no such ground in reality.

"And Elijah came unto all the people, and said, How long halt ye between two opinions? if the Lord be God, follow him: but if Baal, then follow him. And the people answered him not a word." (1 Kings 18:21)

Jesus said "And why call ye me, Lord, Lord, and do not the things which I say? Whosoever cometh to me, and hears my sayings, and does them, I will shew you to whom he is like: He is like a man which built an house, and dug deep, and laid the foundation on a rock: and when the flood arose, the stream beat vehemently upon that house, and could not shake it: for it was founded upon a rock. But he that hears, and does not, is like a man that without a foundation built an house upon the earth; against which the stream did beat vehemently, and immediately it fell; and the ruin of that house was great." (Luke 6:46-49)

"And hereby we do know that we know him, if we keep his commandments. He that saith, I know him, and keeps not his commandments, is a liar, and the truth is not in him. But whoso keeps his word, in him verily is the love of God perfected: hereby know we that we are in him. He that saith he abides in him ought himself also so to walk, even as he walked." (1 John 2:3-6)

True Salvation

True faith is when we are really persuaded that Christ in truth has a right to reign over us and that it is better to go his way no matter what it means for us and whatever it should cost us in this life. Jesus' reign is for our ultimate good when we are subject to him. His going to the cross to die for our sins proved his love and his goodness; so we can trust him with our lives. So trusting him means believing him and keeping his word even if doing so brings loss in terms of earthly possessions, relationships, and/or other things like comforts, goals, dreams, etc believing that he will be faithful ultimately regardless of the present suffering. The Bible guarantees that those who follow him will face tribulation (Acts 14:22) as all who walk contrary to a fierce wind must battle its force. Yet the Bible also says that those who are led by the Lord's rule as their shepherd will have goodness and mercy follow them all the days of their life; and that they'll dwell in the Lord's house forever (Psalm 23:6). **"Man shall not live by bread alone, but by every word that proceeds out of the mouth of God." (Matthew 4:4)**

Here in this (commonly misused) passage from Romans 10 we see the the transfer from darkness to light that is offered to us freely, the richness of God's grace that we can have, on the condition of believing in our heart that Jesus is Lord in truth and thus calling on him and confessing him as Lord. It is true righteousness and our great gain if we will thus believe on Him and receive Him.

"That if thou shalt confess with thy mouth the Lord Jesus, and shalt believe in thine heart that God hath raised him from the dead, thou shalt be saved. For with the heart man believes unto righteousness; and with the mouth confession is made unto salvation. For the scripture saith, Whosoever believes on him shall not be ashamed. For there is no difference between the Jew and the Greek: for the same Lord over all is rich unto all that call upon him. For whosoever shall call upon the name of the Lord shall be saved." (Romans 10:9-13)

The Spirit Of God

All who believe on Jesus in truth are then given the Spirit of God (same as the Spirit of Christ and the Holy Spirit) to dwell in them (Ephesians 1:13). A true gospel salvation is to be a partaker of Christ's life and nature by His Spirit and thus of the power of God which is able to save from the way of death and the sins which God's wrath is against. **"But God commends his love toward us, in that, while we were yet sinners, Christ died for us. Much more then, being now justified by his blood, we shall be saved from wrath through him. For if, when we were enemies, we were reconciled to God by the death of his Son, much more, being reconciled, we shall be saved by his life." (Romans 5:8-10)**

The Spirit of Christ IS the essential of the kingdom of God and thus true Christianity. It's one thing to say we repent and believe in Jesus- but the receiving of the Spirit of God and the Spirit's power continually working in one is God's very own witness that he accepts one's repentance and faith in Christ as being genuinely on His terms. There is no such thing as Christianity without Christ himself, and Christ lives and works in people by his Spirit when he is glorified as Lord.

Peter told the Jewish leaders after Christ's death and resurrection. **"The God of our fathers raised up Jesus, whom ye slew and hanged on a tree. Him hath God exalted with his right hand to be a Prince and a Saviour, for to give repentance to Israel, and forgiveness of sins. And we are his witnesses of these things; and so is also the Holy Ghost, whom God hath given to them that obey him." (Acts 5:30-32)**

"For the kingdom of God is not meat and drink; but righteousness, and peace, and joy in the

Holy Ghost." (Romans 14:17)

"Now if any man have not the Spirit of Christ, he is none of his." (Romans 8:9b)

Seducing Spirits And Avoiding Deception

"Now the Spirit speaks expressly, that in the latter times some shall depart from the faith, giving heed to seducing spirits, and doctrines of devils." (1 Timothy 4:1)

The proceeding verse is a warning from God's Spirit that there other spirits, seducing spirits from the devil, we must beware of that are not the Holy Spirit which can nonetheless imitate the influences of the Holy Spirit and lead people to receive false gospels and thus to worship a false jesus or other false gods. There are events we may see, hear about, or read about where a supernatural work or vision is being promoted with apparently convincing evidence of its supernatural origin. Most people believe that if the event is indeed supernatural/miraculous it must be of God. Not so! Oftentimes the message which comes out of those apparently supernatural encounters is one that is contradictory to God's word and one that leads people away from the Jesus of the Bible and the fear of the Lord.[27] Often a message that promises salvation and hope even to those who continue in willful sin and thus oppose the kingdom of God; a message that gives a (supposed) way to be saved apart from receiving Jesus Christ on his terms; a message where the "jesus" being promoted is a false one that seeks to unite mankind on other terms than

---

[27] The real Jesus of the Bible proclaims the fear of the Lord- scriptures like Mark 9:43-48, Luke 12:4-5 and many others show this.

the truth revealed by the Jesus of the Bible and his cross which calls us to die to self in order to find true life. Demons can even appear as people or heavenly beings in visions/dreams and call themselves "Jesus," "God," "angels," or refer to themselves as notable/familiar people while giving a deceptive message that is completely opposed to the truth in God's word.[28] We must take these scriptures about seducing spirits extremely seriously. They are something which God saw it fit to give us multiple warnings about in His word.

Remember that Jesus himself warned that there would be great deception in the end-times <u>through supernatural/miraculous works</u>. He said **"Then if any man shall say unto you, Lo, here is Christ, or there; believe it not. For there shall arise false Christs, and false prophets, <u>and shall shew great signs and wonders; insomuch that, if it were possible, they shall deceive the very elect</u>. Behold, I have told you before." (Matthew 24:23-25)**

The Apostle Paul wrote to the Corinthian church which he had planted. **"But I fear, lest <u>by any means</u>, as the serpent beguiled Eve through his subtlety, so your minds should be corrupted from the simplicity that is in Christ. For if he that cometh preaches another Jesus, whom we have not preached, or if ye receive another spirit, which ye have not received, or another gospel, which ye have not accepted, ye might well bear with him." (2 Corinthians 11:3-4)** Paul would go on to say **"For such are false apostles, deceitful workers, transforming themselves into the apostles of Christ.**

---

[28]Often strengthening one's conviction in an area they already deceived in. We really need to love the truth of God's word and test *everything* by it in order to not be deceived (2 Thessalonians 2:9-12, 1 Thessalonians 5:21-22).

And no marvel; for Satan himself is transformed into an angel of light. Therefore it is no great thing if his ministers also be transformed as the ministers of righteousness; whose end shall be according to their works." (2 Corinthians 11:13-15)

So how can we know God's Spirit from a seducing spirit? By the test God's word gives us to apply. **"Beloved, believe not every spirit, but try the spirits whether they are of God: because many false prophets are gone out into the world." (1 John 4:1)**

Then we are given this key instruction. **"Hereby know ye the Spirit of God: Every spirit that confesses that Jesus Christ is come in the flesh is of God: And every spirit that confesses not that Jesus Christ is come in the flesh is not of God: and this is that spirit of antichrist, whereof ye have heard that it should come; and even now already is it in the world." (1 John 4:2-3)** This is referring to more than a verbal confession that Jesus Christ is come in the flesh. What deceiving spirits never can do which the Holy Spirit does is give genuine holiness in the heart- they cannot produce the nature of Jesus which in power reveals the righteousness of God and fulfills the righteousness of God's law (Romans 1:16-17, Romans 8:4). The Spirit of God always is forming Christ's character in the one who is living by faith in Christ. The Spirit of God will always direct the one he is leading to consent to Christ's word and to keep it. With this it should be said that anyone whose message contradicts the pure teaching of Jesus and the Apostles is not of God and shouldn't be heeded, as the Holy Spirit cannot/will not contradict the word of God which he inspired (2 Timothy 3:15-17). **"To the law and to the testimony: if they speak not according to this word, it is because there is no light in them." (Isaiah 8:20)**

Not unrelated to this, there are also many groups which might affirm everything in this chapter until to this point, but who ultimately depart from the word of God by equating obedience to Christ with obedience to the group's teachings which in some way take away from and/or add to the word of Christ and his apostles. Thus they are antichrist in nature, as they are a rival to Christ in conflict with him. The Bible teaches about elders with pure lives who lead people by the word of God (Hebrews 13:7);[29] yet many groups are not governed by the word of God but by commandments of men which are given priority over the word of God. Jesus spoke of those who reject the commandment of God in order to keep their own tradition-commandments of men that are suited for those whose hearts are far from God (Mark 7:6-9).[30]

Some groups may make great demands of people which might require even more sacrifice to fulfill than obedience to the word of God would require. Yet ultimately they replace the need to surrender to God and take up the cross to follow Christ for devotion to the

---

[29] See 1 Timothy 3:1-7 and Titus 1:5-9 for the required qualifications of a church leader that God recognizes.

[30] And many groups now even teach we are not obligated to keep any commandments at all. They neglect the truth which is said constantly in the New Testament in various ways: Faith in Christ does not make void the (moral) law of God but rather establishes it (Romans 3:31). This attempt to make void God's law is called antinomianism. Antinomianism wrongly separates faith in Christ from obedience to his commandments; and thus falsely promises salvation to those who continue in willful sin. Beware of it and flee from its influence! And it should be said that even the groups which say we are not obligated to keep God's commandments still have their own traditions which all who would be part of the group must go along with. Those who won't be under Christ's yoke will be in bondage to something/someone else.

group/group leader- and thereby rob people of the life and freedom that only come by death to self through taking up the cross and receiving Christ's reign; and thereby receiving the power of his resurrection life by the Holy Spirit. These groups will read the Bible as those who in Jesus' time who forsook the commandment of God for the commandments of men also read the Bible.[31] Yet ultimately they'll only look at certain passages and explain away what they don't ignore completely by an interpretation of their leader(s) which doesn't hold when/if the interpretation is looked at in light of the entire chapter and/or book the passage is in; and when compared to the rest of the Bible's teaching on the given subject. We have an obligation to search the scriptures daily and diligently to try whether messages we hear, as well as churches/groups we would consider joining (or are already in) align with God's word or not. Any who follow those who deviate from Christ's word will fall into the same ditch they fall into (Luke 6:39). Those who stay in a group that is in conflict with the word of God out of preference for comfort, convenience, or out of fear of man are disobedient to Christ and prefer his enemies over him. The clear command of His word is: **"Whosoever transgresses, and abides not in the doctrine of Christ, hath not God. He that abides in the doctrine** (teaching) **of Christ, he hath both the Father and the Son. If there come any unto you, and bring not this doctrine** (teaching)**, receive him not into your house, neither bid him God speed[32]: For he that bids him God speed is partaker of his evil deeds." (2 John 9-11)**

We are warned that the great deception of the last days is a (counterfeit) form of Christianity without the power to deliver from living in sin (see 2 Timothy 3:1-5).

---

[31]They had the Old Testament/Hebrew Bible in Jesus' time.
[32]Prays for God's blessing on his ministry.

A counterfeit Christianity that sees no conflict between serving self and faith in Christ. A counterfeit Christianity which has many of the elements of the genuine, yet which doesn't insist like Christ and the Apostles did that taking up the cross and dying to selfish ambition is necessary to follow Christ and have eternal life.[33] This deception must be guarded against closely, as it can be subtle. Anyone who says at heart about anything related to breaking God's commandments such as "I know I shouldn't be doing this, but I am anyway," "I know I ought to do that, but I'm not," "This is the way I am, and I won't change," or "I don't really care what God says about this"- anyone who says any of these things <u>at heart</u> is evidently taken by this deception and must therefore repent of disobedience towards Christ and his kingdom. **"Therefore to him that knows to do good, and does it not, to him it is sin." (James 4:17) "Nevertheless the foundation of God stands sure, having this seal, The Lord knows them that are his. And, let every one that names the name of Christ depart from iniquity." (2 Timothy 2:19)**

Enduring In The Faith

It's important to say with what has been said so far regarding the kingdom of God that the Bible also says we must continue in following and confessing Jesus as our Lord and being delivered from sin through a real, saving knowledge of him. Though many emphasize a one-time moment/decision as a permanent fix to the issue of one's eternal salvation, Jesus and the Apostles taught we must pass from death to life through faith in Christ as Lord and Savior and thus continue in that faith as Jesus' disciple until the end of our lives or until Christ's second coming (which ever comes first).

---

[33]See also John 12:24-26, Galatians 2:20, Galatians 6:14-16 etc.

Jesus made it absolutely clear regarding the need to endure in his kingdom as his disciple to the end. **"And many false prophets shall rise, and shall deceive many. And because iniquity shall abound, the love of many shall wax cold. But he that shall endure unto the end, the same shall be saved." (Matthew 24:11-13)**

Jesus did not die for us so we can sin and live carelessly and no longer be held accountable for our thoughts, words, and actions. This truth has been seen from the Bible throughout this book. Having our sins not counted against us in Christ only is only ours in us giving glory to God and no longer justifying/excusing rebellion and works of darkness. **"What shall we say then? Shall we continue in sin, that grace may abound? <u>God forbid</u>.[34] How shall we, that are dead to sin, live any longer therein?" (Romans 6:1-2) "If we say that we have fellowship with him, and walk in darkness, we lie, and do not the truth: But if we walk in the light, as he is in the light, we have fellowship one with another, and the blood of Jesus Christ his Son cleanses us from all sin." (1 John 1:6-7)** Nobody is secure to the point where they are free from their obligations to God and man- and thus from the consequences of not fulfilling them. True security in Christ is not that we are allowed to consent to sin and walk in darkness. True security in Christ is that we do not have to do so because there in all-sufficient Savior whose strong enough to save those under His reign from going astray as He is yielded to and called upon in truth.

Where Jesus reigns over one the righteousness of God's law will be fulfilled in them through his Spirit's power. **"For the kingdom of God is not in word, but in power." (1 Corinthians 4:20).** Overcoming sin from its

---

[34]The plain truth here is that God forbids us from continuing in sin; and therefore grace will not abound for those who do.

root in the heart and not being proud of that victory come through submitting to Christ and calling on him to deliver us and to supply his righteousness by his Spirit. **"For the law of the Spirit of life in Christ Jesus hath made me free from the law of sin and death." (Romans 8:2)** Power doesn't by our own effort and strength but by coming to Christ recognizing that we have nothing, no ability nor power to live righteously in ourselves *as well as* faith to believe that Christ is willing and able to work in us to provide us his power to live in genuine holiness and righteousness as he is submitted to and depended on (see Luke 1:74-75). **"Blessed are the poor in spirit" (Matthew 5:3)** is the first New Covenant principle. All other truths cannot profit us without this poverty of spirit as it is the only way to be given the true riches of Christ.

To continue in subjection to Jesus' word in God's kingdom, and thus enduring in his Spirit's power in overcoming sin's temptation is called "walking after the Spirit;" whereas living after our own desires under sin's dominion is called "walking after the flesh." We have the promise **"This I say then, Walk in the Spirit, and ye shall not fulfill the lust of the flesh." (Galatians 5:16)** We need to obey the command here to walk in the Spirit and believe the accompanying promise since those who turn out of the way of righteousness in Christ to go their own way again deny him and forsake the very essence of salvation (see Titus 1:16 with 2 Peter 2:20-22). We are therefore commanded to watch and be sober repeatedly in the Bible, because sin is always calling us to embrace it. We must therefore continually yield to Christ and call on him to deliver us out of the hand of our ultimate mortal enemy.[35] We are therefore instructed:

---

[35]Satan and the world-system are our mortal enemies too; they are so because they entice us to walk after the flesh and serve sin.

"Let not sin therefore reign in your mortal body, that ye should obey it in the lusts thereof. Neither yield ye your members as instruments of unrighteousness unto sin: but yield yourselves unto God, as those that are alive from the dead, and your members as instruments of righteousness unto God. For sin shall not have dominion over you: for ye are not under the law, but under grace. What then? shall we sin, because we are not under the law, but under grace? God forbid. Know ye not, that to whom ye yield yourselves servants to obey, his servants ye are to whom ye obey; whether of sin unto death, or of obedience unto righteousness?" (Romans 6:12-16)

"But he giveth more grace. Wherefore he saith, God resists the proud, but giveth grace unto the humble. Submit yourselves therefore to God. Resist the devil, and he will flee from you. Draw nigh to God, and he will draw nigh to you. Cleanse your hands, ye sinners; and purify your hearts, ye double minded. Be afflicted, and mourn, and weep: let your laughter be turned to mourning, and your joy to heaviness. Humble yourselves in the sight of the Lord, and he shall lift you up." (James 4:6-10)

We see from Romans 6:12-16 and James 4:6-10 previously quoted that sin and Satan will not have dominion/power over the one under the grace of God; and that the faith which causes one to be under God's grace is exercised by the means of humbly submitting to God as one identifying with Christ in his death to sin and his being alive to God. When faith and grace are thus understood as the Bible defines them we can see how obeying Christ's commandments and overcoming temptation are gifts of God that are freely offered to us in Christ. It is not about us "getting the job done" but about holding onto Christ and not departing from him. **"That as sin hath reigned unto death, even so might grace reign through righteousness unto eternal life by Jesus Christ our Lord." (Romans 5:21)**

We are thus told: **"As ye have therefore received Christ Jesus the Lord, so walk ye in him" (Colossians 2:6)**- This scripture shows that we are to walk in Christ as we should first come to him. That is to come <u>to him</u> as Lord in complete reliance on him to deliver us from sin's power, wash us from our sins by his blood, and lead us in his way. We can be forgiven and restored if we are overtaken by sin yet THIS is how we must so come back if we go astray from him. **"Seeing then that we have a great high priest, that is passed into the heavens, Jesus the Son of God, let us hold fast our profession. For we have not an high priest which cannot be touched with the feeling of our infirmities; but was in all points tempted like as we are, yet without sin. Let us therefore come boldly unto the throne of grace, that we may obtain mercy, and find grace to help in time of need." (Hebrews 4:14-16)**

"Rooted and built up in him, and established in the faith, as ye have been taught, abounding therein with thanksgiving." (Colossians 2:7)- Thus in the way we first come to him we are also told to be rooted and built up in our walk with him by holding onto him for dear life and seeking growth through knowing him more, established in the faith[36] and continually thanking God for his redemption and deliverance He has provided in Christ; and thus the victory that can be ours in every situation as well as the mercies He has already given. The early disciple Barnabas upon meeting new believers in Christ

---

[36] Which is abiding in teachings of Christ and the Apostles- 2 John 9.

"exhorted them all, that with purpose of heart they would cleave (hold fast) **unto the Lord." (Acts 11:23b)**

"Beware lest any man spoil you through philosophy and vain deceit, after the tradition of men, after the rudiments (principles) **of the world, and not after Christ. For in him dwells all the fulness of the Godhead bodily." (Colossians 2:8-9)**- We are warned about being spoiled (ruined) by seeking stability and growth in the philosophies of men and false teachings that do not line up with the word of Christ and the Apostles. These things ultimately ruin those who go after them. We are commanded not to (and do not need to) go to teachings outside of the word of God and teachings that explain away what the word of God clearly says <u>in order to be right with Him and to grow in Christ</u>. An example would be someone who says they have understanding that isn't in the Bible but (they say) is nevertheless necessary to know to be a victorious Christian. Another example would be those who say you must (or must not) eat or drink something or must observe a certain holy-day to be right with God. These things ultimately turn those who heed them away from Christ; in whom those that are united to him by faith are indeed complete (Colossians 2:10).

The Triumph Of Christ's Kingdom

The world is heading towards the day when Jesus will back in great power and glory. He will put down all opposition to him and take his power over the world that rightfully belongs to him. Then the present kingdom of God that is now in Christ's people choosing to glorify him by following him in obedience from the heart, though it involves suffering, will then be revealed before all creation in glory. Paul told the Christians in Rome about those whom God's Spirit bears witness to in the present that they are indeed God's children: **"And if children, then heirs;**

heirs of God, and joint-heirs with Christ; if so be that we suffer with him, that we may be also glorified together. For I reckon that the sufferings of this present time are not worthy to be compared with the glory which shall be revealed in us." (Romans 8:17-18)

At Christ's second coming all rebellion to him will be put down. **"The Lord said unto my Lord, Sit thou at my right hand, until I make thine enemies thy footstool." (Psalm 110:1)** Those who have refused his righteous reign will not be able to stand and will face his just wrath as those who have no part in him and in the benefits provided by his death on the cross (Romans 2:4-5). Christ's reign will be eternal and thus the consequences of being ready or not for the day of his coming are eternal. Then the consequences of receiving or rejecting Christ's righteous reign will be demonstrated and experienced.

"Blessed is the man that endures temptation: for when he is tried, he shall receive the crown of life, which the Lord hath promised to them that love him." (James 1:12)

"The lofty looks of man shall be humbled, and the haughtiness of men shall be bowed down, and the Lord alone shall be exalted in that day." (Isaiah 2:11)

"The Lord Jesus shall be revealed from heaven with his mighty angels, In flaming fire taking vengeance on them that know not God, and that obey not the gospel of our Lord Jesus Christ: Who shall be punished with everlasting destruction from the presence of the Lord, and from the glory of his power; When he shall come to be glorified in his saints, and to be admired in all them that believe" (2 Thessalonians 1:7b-10a)

"Then cometh the end, when he shall have delivered up the kingdom to God, even the Father; when he shall have put down all rule and all authority and power. For he must reign, till he hath put all enemies under his feet. The last enemy that shall be destroyed is death. For he hath put all things under his feet. But when he saith all things are put under him, it is manifest (obvious) that he is excepted, which did put all things under him. And when all things shall be subdued unto him, then shall the Son also himself be subject unto him that put all things under him, that God may be all in all." (1 Corinthians 15:24-28)

"And the seventh angel sounded; and there were great voices in heaven, saying, The kingdoms of this world are become the kingdoms of our Lord, and of his Christ; and he shall reign for ever and ever. And the four and twenty elders, which sat before God on their seats, fell upon their faces, and worshipped God, Saying, We give thee thanks, O Lord God Almighty, which art, and wast, and art to come; because thou hast taken to thee thy great power, and hast reigned. And the nations were angry, and thy wrath is come, and the time of the dead, that they should be judged, and that thou shouldest give reward unto thy servants the prophets, and to the saints, and them that fear thy name, small and great; and shouldest destroy them which destroy (i.e. corrupt) the earth." (Revelation 11:15-18)

Chapter 5:
Sobriety: An Essential Of True Christianity

An incredibly great factor for us regarding entering and staying on the way that leads to life is that of sobriety. A continual consideration of Christ's coming as the judge of all mankind and the eternal consequences thereof which will be rendered by our response to him (and thus to his word) is crucial. Taking this consideration seriously, along with considering the very reason Christ gave himself for our sins, and responding to these in an appropriate manner necessarily brings up the issue of sobriety.

"For the grace of God that brings salvation hath appeared to all men, Teaching us that, denying ungodliness and worldly lusts, we should live soberly, righteously, and godly, in this present world. Looking for that blessed hope, and the glorious appearing of the great God and our Saviour Jesus Christ; Who gave himself for us, that he might redeem us from all iniquity, and purify unto himself a peculiar people, zealous of good works." (Titus 2:11-14)

If we are taught of the grace of God that brings salvation we will be learning to deny ungodliness and worldly lusts and to live soberly, righteously, and godly in this present world in preparation for Christ's second coming. By the above verses it's clear that true

Christianity and the grace of God can't be separated from sobriety; and having sobriety is essential for every aspect of the Christian walk.

The Basis For Sobriety

Olympic athletes train and prepare for the day when their performance will be put on display before the whole world. The Olympic events themselves reveal the effort and effectiveness of their training and preparation. An athlete who is wise will make all their decisions as a preparation for "that day" when they are put on trial before all. They will prepare their body through proper diet, exercise, rest, etc- as well as train their mind to focus on the task at hand and not get distracted. They will also (if they are wise) not do anything that will hinder their training and their overall health. Those who subject themselves to this "restricted lifestyle" do so because they are preparing for a day which has such great importance to them that whatever they must do that makes them uncomfortable and whatever pleasure/comfort that they must deny themselves have such small value compared to being ready and not ashamed on "that day."

The truth then is that we all have a day coming when our whole lives and the secrets of our hearts[37] will be put on trial not merely before billions of people and millions of angels, but above all before God Himself! We have seen throughout this book that the gospel of Christ's purpose is to save us from that way of life and those things which God's wrath is against so we can actually be worthy of his eternal kingdom that is characterized by genuine holiness and righteousness. The ultimate end of living in alignment with this purpose is an eternal glory that comes by what God has done in us through Christ as we have

---

[37]See Romans 2:16

subjected ourselves to him and have believed his promises that we **"might be partakers of the divine nature, having escaped the corruption that is in the world through lust."** (see **2 Peter 1:4)**. Thus we see how Jesus in giving the call of the gospel to eternal life and its conditions made the day of judgment and the eternal consequences of our choices a motivation to be diligent to heed his words.

"Then said Jesus unto his disciples, If any man will come after me, let him deny himself, and take up his cross, and follow me. For whosoever will save his life shall lose it: and whosoever will lose his life for my sake shall find it. For what is a man profited, if he shall gain the whole world, and lose his own soul? or what shall a man give in exchange for his soul? For the Son of man shall come in the glory of his Father with his angels; and then he shall reward every man according to his works." (Matthew 16:24-27)

Preparing for the judgment is in itself a matter of faith for **"faith is the substance of things hoped for, the evidence of things not seen." (Hebrews 11:1)** By truly believing what God has testified in the Bible about judgment day we should be just as persuaded about the reality of our "event" in meeting the Lord of the Universe as Olympic athletes are regarding the reality of their event and the importance of its outcome (which outcome is nothing compared to the outcome of judgment day). In simply reading the gospels it's clear that Christ spoke much about judgment day, eternity, hell, and God's eternal kingdom- so if we believe him we'll be diligent in seeking God so that we are ready to meet Him. We see shortly after in Hebrews 11 the relation between faith and coming judgment from the example given of Noah. **"But without faith it is impossible to please him: for he that cometh to God must believe that he is, and that he is a** rewarder of them that diligently seek him. By faith Noah, <u>being warned of God of things not seen as yet, moved with fear, prepared</u> an ark to the saving of his house; by the which he condemned the world, and became heir of the righteousness which is by faith." (Hebrews 11:6-7)

"Wherefore gird up the loins of your mind, be sober, and hope to the end for the grace that is to be brought unto you at the revelation of Jesus Christ; As obedient children, not fashioning yourselves according to the former lusts in your ignorance: But as he which hath called you is holy, so be ye holy in all manner of conversation (living); Because it is written, Be ye holy; for I am holy." (1 Peter 1:13-16)

We see here from the book of 1 Peter that sobriety or the lack thereof has its foundation in the mind. Holiness (true holiness that is) is being set apart from the lustful corruption in the world to obey God and do His will. We can't say we want to do God's will but hold onto to certain things we take pleasure in that displease Him. Even things that aren't sinful in and of themselves need to be laid on the altar to be modified or maybe even given up if they are a hindrance to living for Christ and bearing a testimony for him in the world. Those that say "Oh, what's the big deal about this? And what's the big deal about that?" need to realize that we are commanded to consider our ways carefully in everything and discern what is pleasing to the Lord because there is no other life to prepare to meet our God but this one.

"Let us hear the conclusion of the whole matter: Fear God, and keep his commandments: for this is the whole duty of man. For God shall bring every work into judgment, with every secret thing, whether it be good, or whether it be evil." (Ecclesiastes

12:13-14) Even if something seems perfectly okay to do why not analyze it from God's word and seek wisdom as to whether it is really something that is good in His eyes? **"The fear of the Lord is the beginning of wisdom: and the knowledge of the holy is understanding." (Proverbs 9:10)** Only those who are utterly serious and careful about living a life that God approves of will rightly have insight into what's acceptable to Him anyway. Those who don't fear the Lord can't have true wisdom and will be deceived by their own hearts which they are set on walking after.

"And if ye call on the Father, who without respect of persons judges according to every man's work, pass the time of your sojourning here in fear: Forasmuch as ye know that ye were not redeemed with corruptible things, as silver and gold, from your vain conversation (living) **received by tradition from your fathers; But with the precious blood of Christ, as of a lamb without blemish and without spot" (1 Peter 1:17-19)**

With that, we must fear in consideration of the awesome and tremendous price Christ paid to redeem us and be utterly concerned that redemption price is not paid in vain in regards to ourselves. One man named Leonard Ravenhill who emphasized in his preaching the necessity of living a sober, wholehearted life for Christ [38] has inscribed on his tombstone a monumental question we do well to answer honestly and deal with seriously. *"Are the things you're living for worth Christ dying for?"*

Spiritual Drunkenness

In the natural realm being drunk is the opposite of

---

[38] And whom we have reason to believe preached only that which he also genuinely lived.

being sober. Both in the natural and spiritual realm drunkenness is a great sin because purposing or risking to be in a state of drunkenness despises God as well as other people by displaying no care or fear of displeasing God as well as no care or fear of doing or saying something that would harm others (as well as a disregard of one's own safety and dignity too). As drunkards in the natural realm willingly deprive themselves of the full use their God-given reason and ability to make appropriate judgments and carry them out- so the spiritual drunkard is careless of how they **"ought to walk and to please God." (see 1 Thessalonians 4:1)**. There is such a thing as being drunk with the pleasures and cares of life and thus to live in disregard of God's truth and insensible to the true condition of one's soul. Jesus gave warnings about drunkenness leading to people's damnation and by reading those warnings and the Bible as a whole those are certainly references to something more than (but including) physical drunkenness (examples in Matthew 24:48-51, Luke 21:34).

Another scary fact is that one who is drunk usually thinks that they are okay and feels confident in their own abilities when they are in reality incompetent- and will even confidently attempt things they'd never attempt if they were sober. Going against God's truth and breaking His commandments is an obvious sign of being spiritually drunk, as well as a careless confidence in one's own ability to know and do what's right (in contrast to the broken, dependent attitude that leans on Christ constantly that can only exist in a sober person). The sober one will look to know what's acceptable to God constantly in every situation while the drunkard isn't concerned because it doesn't matter to him or he just presumes he knows. **"And Jesus said, For judgment I am come into this world, that they which see not might see; and that they which see might be made blind." (John 9:39)**

As in the natural realm, so in the spiritual realm those who evidence any sign of drunkenness usually have a sense of false security. While the sober, watchful person can have a true safety and security, the drunkard feels very safe and secure <u>even though he shouldn't because he isn't safe at all.</u> A spiritually sober person who lives in preparation for judgment day and eternity will either have a true security in an obedient relationship with the Lord or will at least know that they aren't safe and will be earnestly seeking to settle all controversies with God to have such a relationship. The spiritual drunkard is confident he won't end up in hell even though he doesn't take sin against God seriously or listen to what the Bible says about hell and how to escape it, <u>which in itself are characteristics of one who is headed for hell</u>.

"Happy is the man that fears always: but he that hardens his heart shall fall into mischief." (Proverbs 28:14)

"Correction is grievous unto him that forsakes the way: and he that hates reproof shall die." (Proverbs 15:10)

Sobering Up To Prepare For Eternity

A real life example of sobering up I know about is when a man who had been careless about the Lord and his own soul saw a close relative on her deathbed. He said upon seeing that it truly hit him that one day the Lord would either say to him **"Well done, good and faithful servant" (Matthew 25:23)** or **"I know you not whence ye are; depart from me, all ye workers of iniquity." (Luke 13:27)** He may not have quoted the verses perfectly, but he referenced them for sure. He knew then that there were things in his life that needed to change and were necessary for him to deal with the Lord about.

The following verse shows the terrible awakening of those who refused to sober up over judgment day/eternity and turn to the Lord while they had the chance. **"The harvest is past, the summer is ended, and we are not saved." (Jeremiah 8:20)** Thus sobriety is necessary to prepare ourselves to meet the Lord, which is what our best interest is and the best interest of others in our lives (if our preparation is indeed according to the instructions in the word of God). This is why it is essential <u>to be taught</u> constantly in the word of God, to come to God's word to understand His will, to be reproved and corrected as need be, and to be instructed how to prepare our heart and live in the truth of Christ. Those who won't come to the word of God regularly, and even those that do but aren't interested in actually hearing from God and thus changing show pride and a lack of sobriety in preparing to meet the Lord. The one who is humble and sober trembles at the word of God, taking to heart how He is awesome beyond words and the terror which comes in accountability to Him. The God who created the vast Universe and knows each one of trillions upon trillions of stars (Psalm 147:4-5) is the God **"with whom we have to do." (Hebrews 4:13) "Let all the earth fear the Lord: let all the inhabitants of the world stand in awe of him. For he spake, and it was done; he commanded, and it stood fast." (Psalm 33:8-9)**

There is a lesson along these lines in the Proverb **"Prepare thy work without, and make it fit for thyself in the field; and afterwards build thine house." (Proverbs 24:27)**

A farmer who relies on crops for his income and/or source of food builds his house around a field that is fit and ready to bring forth an abundance of crops when he is wise. He doesn't do the opposite and build a house first and then examine the quality of the soil in the field around the house afterward. <u>He secures that which is absolutely necessary before he attends to other things that are secondary in relation to that absolutely necessary thing</u>. So we should take care that all we do in this life (work, friendships, marriage, other activities, etc) are built around what is wise from an eternal prospective and thus a faith that values Christ above all else. No resolve or commitment to be a true Christian and keep Christ's word will stand unless the issue of Christ's value above all else is positively decided without any conditions (see Luke 14:16-33). That is a faith which puts the most necessary priority of being Christ's disciple and thus hearing his word and keeping it (Luke 10:41-42, Luke 11:28) as that which everything else is secondary to and which wins out over our own natural desires and the desires of other people; even those of our closest friends and relatives which would require us to compromise God's truth if given into.

In relation to this we are told to **"Buy the truth, and sell *it* not; also wisdom, and instruction, and understanding." (Proverbs 23:23)**

To **"buy the truth"** refers to more than just reading the Bible, though that is certainly included in this statement. It means to go to any length to really understand the truth and walk in Christ's commandments (2 John 4, 6) when we are certain how we must apply them in our lives (and if we are set on walking in the truth we'll genuinely seek this application in sincerity without self-imposed conditions- see Proverbs 3:5-8). To **"sell *it* not"** likewise means not to forsake walking in God's truth for anything/anyone at all after we have bought it.

The Apostle Paul gave the following instruction

for us to help us avoid the great danger that we all are in of being overly concerned with and/or consumed by the gains and the losses, the joy and the heartbreak, etc of this life. **"But this I say, brethren, the time is short: it remains, that both they that have wives be as though they had none; And they that weep, as though they wept not; and they that rejoice, as though they rejoiced not; and they that buy, as though they possessed not; And they that use this world, as not abusing it: for the fashion of this world passes away." (1 Corinthians 7:29-31)** In consideration of judgment day and eternity all the different circumstances of this life are so short and insignificant that, no matter how wonderful or horrible they may be, they are still not significant enough to let them distract us from preparing for judgment day/eternity and thus seeking the kingdom of God above all else. All will surely realize on judgment day what indeed ought to have been the undisputed top priority in this life.

We do well to think about what it would be like to actually stand before God on the day of judgment. Would not one who didn't prepare like they ought to have then want to go back and have a second chance to make things right? Yet there will be no second chance, no "do-over" when we die or when Christ comes back. **"And as it is appointed unto men once to die, but after this the judgment." (Hebrews 9:27)** Now we actually *do* have the chance to prepare and walk in the truth with our whole hearts- as multitudes will wish on judgment day that they had a chance to go back and live life over in order to do- *but won't be able to*.

Now there is a chance for us to prepare to meet God and to help others to prepare to meet Him. Now is **"the acceptable year of the Lord"** before **"the day of vengeance of our God"** (see **Isaiah 61:2**). The brightness of God's patience and offer of mercy now lighten the world as a rainbow- yet will also fade away as all rainbows do.

Now the way to life is prepared by Christ and all who would be saved from the way of the world and its corruption can enter this way through the door that is Jesus Christ and follow him to eternal glory. Those who are with him on this way and that which he has done in them and through them will stand when the heavens and the earth are shaken and all that is of man will crumble and be brought down forever.

"And the kings of the earth, and the great men, and the rich men, and the chief captains, and the mighty men, and every bondman, and every free man, hid themselves in the dens and in the rocks of the mountains; And said to the mountains and rocks, Fall on us, and hide us from the face of him that sits on the throne, and from the wrath of the Lamb: For the great day of his wrath is come; and who shall be able to stand?" (Revelation 6:15-17)

Thus we are told before that day arrives: **"And now, little children, abide in him** (Christ); **that, when he shall appear, we may have confidence, and not be ashamed before him at his coming." (1 John 2:28)**

"But the end of all things is at hand: be ye therefore sober, and watch unto prayer." (1 Peter 4:7)

Books by Aaron Carey:

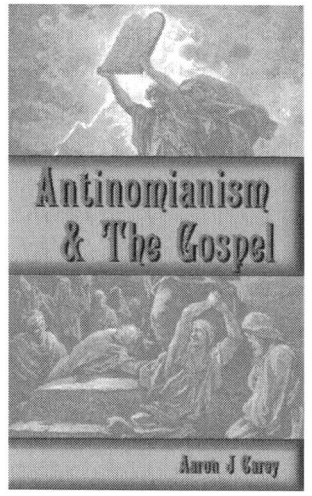 

For additional copies of **The Way to Life** or to receive a copy of Antinomianism and the Gospel please contact us, or ask your local bookseller to stock titles from Apprehending Truth Publishers.

Also available at your favorite online bookseller.

Look for these titles in your favorite eBook format.

Titles published by Apprehending Truth:

Understanding Misunderstood Texts of Scripture
Asa Mahan, J. L. Wallace

Defining Biblical Holiness
John Wesley, Asa Mahan

The Works of John Fletcher:
Volume I: Five Checks To Antinomianism

Antinomianism and the Gospel by Aaron Carey
The Way To Life by Aaron Carey

What the Bible Really Teaches About Divorce and Remarriage by Mark Bullen
Did Jesus Correct Moses? by Mark Bullen
God's Crucible by Mark Bullen

Titles to be Released in 2013
Apprehending Truth
Deceptions of Rome
Debating Islam
The Works of John Fletcher:
Volume II: Creeds and Scripture Scales
Volume III: Doctrines of Grace and Justice

See our website for details

---

www.publishers.apprehendingtruth.net
Buy the Truth and sell it not. ~ Proverbs xxiii, 23

Made in the USA
Charleston, SC
10 February 2013